START & RUN A
HANDYMAN BUSINESS

START & RUN A HANDYMAN BUSINESS

Sarah White and Kevin Pegg

Self-Counsel Press
(a division of)
International Self-Counsel Press Ltd.
USA   Canada

Self-Counsel Press acknowledges the financial support of the Government of Canada through the Book Publishing Industry Development Program (BPIDP) for our publishing activities.

Printed in Canada

First edition: 2005

Library and Archives Canada Cataloguing in Publication

White, Sarah (Sarah Anne)
    Start & run a handyman business / Sarah White and Kevin Pegg.
--1st ed.

    (Self-counsel business series)
    ISBN 1-55180-598-7

1. Repairing trades--Management. 2. New business enterprises--Management. I. Pegg, Kevin II. Title. III. Title: Start and run a handyman business. IV. Series.

TH4815.W44 2005   643'.7'068   C2005-900267-0

Self-Counsel Press
(a division of)
International Self-Counsel Press Ltd.

1704 North State Street	1481 Charlotte Road
Bellingham, WA 98225	North Vancouver, BC V7J 1H1
USA	Canada

We'd like to dedicate this book to our children,
Graham and Heather, and to Morag White.

CONTENTS

INTRODUCTION   xv

1   THE HANDYMAN BUSINESS: AN OPPORTUNITY WAITING FOR YOU   1

    1. What a Handyman Does   1

    2. Do You Have What It Takes?   2

    3. Advantages and Disadvantages   4

    4. Part Time or Full Time?   4

       4.1   Part time   6

       4.2   Full time   6

2   GETTING STARTED   9

    1. Your Goals and Expectations   9

    2. Sizing Up the Market   10

       2.1   Market size   10

	2.2	Market research	11
	2.3	Facing the competition	12
	3.	Developing Your Business Plan	12
	4.	Business and Legal Requirements	13
	4.1	Zoning and licensing	13
	4.2	Form of business	16
	4.3	Insurance	16
	4.4	Naming your business	17
	4.5	Hiring employees or contract staff	18
	5.	Accounting Basics	19
	5.1	Bookkeeping	19
	5.2	Your balance sheet	19
	5.3	Tax requirements	20
	6.	Getting Professional Help for Your Business	20

3 SETTING UP SHOP — 23

1.	Getting Organized	23
2.	Your Home Headquarters	24
2.1	Keeping records	24
2.2	Communication needs	27
2.3	Your office environment	29
2.4	Tax advantages to the home office	30
2.5	Keeping your home and office separate	31
3.	Your Vehicle — An Office Away from Home	32
3.1	Van, truck, or car?	32
3.2	Using trailers and wagons	33
3.3	Vehicle supplies	34
4.	Tools — The Handyman's Best Friend	36
4.1	A basic tool kit	36
4.2	The right tools for the job	38

4 MARKETING YOUR BUSINESS — 41

| 1. | Letterhead and Business Cards | 41 |
| 2. | Word of Mouth | 42 |

	3.	Advertising	43
	4.	Build on Existing Clients	43
	5.	Networking	46
	6.	Marketing Tips	52

5	**MEETING THE CUSTOMER'S NEEDS**	53
	1.	Estimates, Quotes, and Pricing	53
		1.1 Understanding quotes and estimates	54
		1.2 What to charge	57
		1.3 Invoicing	58
	2.	Scheduling	59
		2.1 Planning for a job	59
	3.	Organizing the Work Site	62
	4.	Serving Your Customers Well	64
	5.	Dealing with Difficult Situations	66
		5.1 Not getting paid	66
		5.2 Damaged property	67
		5.3 Family arguments	68
		5.4 Unhappy customers	68
	6.	When There Is Too Much Work	69
		6.1 Saying no to work	69
		6.2 Hiring help	70
	7.	Summary — The Key to Customer Service	71

6	**THE HANDYMAN AT WORK: ON-THE-JOB TIPS AND TECHNIQUES**	73
	1.	Doing the Right Job at the Right Time	73
	2.	Working on New Homes	75
	3.	Working on Older Homes	75
	4.	Painting Like a Pro	76
		4.1 Painting preparation	77
		4.2 Oil or latex?	77
		4.3 How much paint will you need?	78
		4.4 Cleanup tips	79

	5.	Working with Plaster and Drywall	79
	6.	Plumbing Pointers	82
	7.	Rules for Roofing	82
	8.	Yard Work	84
	9.	Taking on Wildlife	85
		9.1 Removing animals	86
		9.2 Pest prevention	88

7 KEEPING UP WITH TRENDS — SOME IDEAS FOR TODAY'S MARKET — 89

	1.	Accessibility and Universal Design	90
	2.	Home Energy Audits	90
	3.	Home Checkups	92
	4.	Home Security	92
	5.	Keeping on Top of Trends	99

8 BUILDING SAFETY AND QUALITY INTO YOUR DAY — 101

	1.	Using Safety Equipment	101
	2.	Assessing the Situation for Safety Concerns	102
	3.	The Safety of Your Customers	104
	4.	A Word about Ladders	105
	5.	Taking Care of Yourself	107
		5.1 Staying fit and safe	107
		5.2 Taking time off	108

9 LOOKING TO THE FUTURE — 111

CHECKLISTS

1	Business Plan Outline	15
2	Home Energy Audit	93
3	Home Checkup	95

ILLUSTRATION

| 1 | Learn to Lift Correctly | 109 |

SAMPLES

1	Business Plan for Goals and Measurables	14
2	Balance Sheet	21
3	Business Card	42
4	Flyer Sample (1)	44
5	Flyer Sample (2)	44
6	Seasonal Reminder Flyer	45
7	Yellow Pages Advertisement	45
8	Community Newspaper Advertisement	46
9	Customer Contact Form	47
10	Customer Follow-Up Note (1)	48
11	Customer Follow-Up Note (2)	49
12	Network Contact Form	51
13	Estimate Sheet	55
14	Service Invoice	60
15	Job Organization Form	61
16	Weekly Work Schedule	63

TABLES

1	The Handyman Business: Pros and Cons	5
2	What Paint for What Job	78
3	Paint Coverage	80
4	Home Security Solutions	98
5	Safety Equipment and When to Use It	103
6	Ladder Guide	105

WORKSHEETS

1	Is the Handyman Business Right for You?	3
2	Tools and Materials Inventory	26

ACKNOWLEDGMENTS

For their help in making sure we had time to complete this book, we'd like to thank Ron, Joyce, Don, Pat, and Jen. For encouragement and enthusiasm, thanks to Jeff, Rob, Susan, Sarah's workmates, Kevin's wonderful customers, and our friends and family.

INTRODUCTION

There is no denying that service businesses are needed more than ever today. It seems everyone is busier than ever with extended workdays, multiple family responsibilities, and other demands on their time. Families of all sizes want to enjoy their free time as they see fit, and for many that means choosing leisure time over the stress of the endless household maintenance tasks required to keep a home running smoothly. Yet most people still want order and functionality, and they recognize the need to keep their homes and property in good working order. The answer for many busy people today is to turn to a handyman to get the job done.

This book is written for anyone who would like to take advantage of the growing need for handyman services and turn it into a viable business. It is also written for those who are thinking of working as a handyman part time, perhaps to earn some extra income or simply to enjoy helping others do those things they cannot or do not want to do themselves. The book is premised on you, the reader, having some skills and experience in solving household

Being a handyman can be full of adventure.

maintenance problems. By adding a few professional techniques and a business strategy offered in this book, you will be well on your way to starting and running a successful, independent handyman business.

Operating your own business requires self-motivation, perseverance, discipline, and common sense. It also requires some business knowledge, and that's where this book can be of particular help. It offers advice on starting up — from registering a business name to customer service considerations to choosing the right equipment. You add the ingredients of your skills and knowledge and your desire to succeed.

Being a handyman can be full of adventure. It brings you in touch with many kinds of people and their homes. It lets you be a problem solver, a creative thinker, and a valuable person to have around. And who wouldn't find satisfaction in being such a person?

We bring to this book our personal experiences and successes. As a working couple with two small children, we know the demands of family life and home ownership. And we have personal experience in both business and handyman work.

Kevin has been a handyman for more than 20 years, offering a wide range of services. He has helped his long-term customers through several home renovations and family changes. Kevin's work experience started early. At the age of 12, he helped on the farm close to his home. He developed a wide range of skills and gradually gained confidence as he learned new ones. As a teenager, Kevin worked at the Pioneer Museum Village in Greenwood, Ontario, providing maintenance services. He specifically learned about the upkeep and maintenance required for historic buildings. After leaving high school, he worked with his father in the family business doing home renovations, painting, and other handyman jobs. During this time he learned to think on his feet, and he became well known for his problem-solving skills. His father had a knack for knowing how to fix anything, and he taught Kevin everything he knew. Kevin carries on the family business today.

Sarah has provided the business background to this book. She assists Kevin in his business by organizing the home office, doing the taxes, and taking care of advertising. She also works full time in the municipal government. Sarah, Kevin, and their children share a 100-year-old home that has been under some form of renovation for more than ten years.

The handyman business has been good to us. As an independent businessman, Kevin can make decisions about how much time he works, how much he is paid, and what kind of work he wants to take on. He is also able to make a good living by helping people improve their homes.

Now we both want to pass on what we have learned. If your goal is to turn your ability to help others improve their homes and lives into a business that also serves you, then this book is for you. To achieve your goal, think and plan carefully. The principles of running a successful handyman business are the same as those needed for running any other enterprise: good judgment and a willingness to work hard. You can reach all your goals if you stay creative, keep learning, and believe in yourself.

Chapter 1

THE HANDYMAN BUSINESS: AN OPPORTUNITY WAITING FOR YOU

1. What a Handyman Does

First and foremost, handymen (and women) are those skilled individuals who can solve problems. Generally their services are geared to home owners who need small jobs done around the house, such as fixing a leaky faucet, installing a light fixture, repairing drywall, or cleaning out a garage. Depending on the skill and ability of the handyman, other services may be offered, such as painting, snow removal, yard work, assembling furniture or equipment, laying carpet, removing junk, or just about anything else you can think of!

The most successful handymen have a wide range of knowledge to draw upon. If you want to start up a handyman business, you should be prepared to work in many areas, including the following:

- Electrical
- Plumbing
- Carpentry

You'll need to be prepared to be called on to do any number of tasks.

- Refinishing surfaces
- Furniture restoration
- Mechanical
- Painting
- Tiling
- Carpet laying
- Drywall

It is also helpful if you have experience working with other tradespeople and you understand when a licensed tradesperson is needed. In other words, you need to know what your limits are.

If you're reading this book, you likely already have the skill to carry out jobs in many, if not most, of these areas. You'll need to be prepared to be called on to do any number of other tasks, as well, depending on your customers' needs. That, simply, is the nature of the handyman business, and it is what makes a handyman so valuable.

2. Do You Have What It Takes?

To run a successful handyman business, you need more than the skills listed above. There are many people who can fix things and pick up the odd job, but without some basic business skills and personal traits, your handyman business will not be truly successful. Take the time to complete Worksheet 1 now to help you in your assessment of your business idea.

Starting a business is easy. But making and keeping it successful are the tricky parts. Success in business requires basic know-how. So, on top of your handyman skills, to keep things running smoothly you need to be able to do the following:

- Keep accurate financial records for accounting and tax purposes
- Organize customer information
- Organize your time and work schedule
- Understand basic marketing and advertising principles and practices
- Practise good communication skills

WORKSHEET 1
IS THE HANDYMAN BUSINESS RIGHT FOR YOU?

Answer the following questions honestly. Knowing yourself and how prepared you are to run your own business are key to your success.

1. Are you able to diagnose and fix most household problems? ❏ yes ❏ no

2. Are you often asked by neighbors and friends for advice on fixing things? ❏ yes ❏ no

3. Do you enjoy the challenge of repairing things around the home? ❏ yes ❏ no

4. Can you organize yourself to get a job done? ❏ yes ❏ no

5. Are you able to do physical work? ❏ yes ❏ no

6. Do you have the tools, vehicle, and home space necessary to run a home-based business? ❏ yes ❏ no

7. Are you willing and able to market yourself and your business? ❏ yes ❏ no

8. Can you work on your own, with little supervision? ❏ yes ❏ no

9. Do you enjoy working with all kinds of people? ❏ yes ❏ no

10. Are you a creative problem-solver? ❏ yes ❏ no

11. Can you accept criticism? ❏ yes ❏ no

12. Can you learn new things and apply them? ❏ yes ❏ no

13. Can you read instructions and use them? ❏ yes ❏ no

14. Are you willing and able to get help as you need it? ❏ yes ❏ no

Think carefully about what you want for your business.

⚒ Learn new things

⚒ Keep interested in business

⚒ Be self-motivated

⚒ Be trustworthy, honest, and respectful

That expertise, the knowledge and skills to meet challenges and problems and overcome them, is necessary for anyone planning a business venture. The good news is that you can learn almost everything you need to know. You can learn from this book, you can learn from talking with other successful businesspeople, you can take courses, and you can read other manuals. The Internet offers a world of knowledge; stores run do-it-yourself seminars; TV shows provide information on home renovations, organization, and maintenance; and self-help tapes and DVDs are available at your local library. The sources of information are almost endless. And, of course, professional help in areas such as accounting and legal advice are available when you need them (see section **6.** of chapter 2).

Your first step is to think carefully about what you want for your business. If you decide that starting a handyman business is for you, the next step is to take action to ensure your goals become reality. A clear understanding of the risks and rewards of running your own business is a good place to start your thinking process.

3. Advantages and Disadvantages

The handyman business, like any business, has its upsides and its downsides. As a handyman, you will work fairly independently, set your own hours, and choose your own customers. But you will also be responsible for finding your own work, estimating how long it takes, and dealing with a new boss (your customer) with every job.

Let's compare the pros and cons of running your own handyman business, shown in Table 1.

4. Part Time or Full Time?

The wonderful thing about having your own business is how flexible it can be. As the owner of your business you can decide when, where, and on what you will work. You will also decide for whom and for how much money. The key is finding the right balance of working the way you want and making enough money to meet your goals.

TABLE 1
THE HANDYMAN BUSINESS: PROS AND CONS

ADVANTAGES	DISADVANTAGES
Can work independently	Solely responsible for work
Can set your own hours	Must be able to cope with both slack times and over-busy times
Can set your own pay (don't need to ask for a raise)	Must sell yourself and your skills to every new customer
Can run the business the way you want to	Must run your business as well as do all the handyman work
Can work from a home office; no need to invest in retail or warehouse space	Family life may be disrupted by home office environment
Do the work you enjoy	Must look for jobs all the time
Opportunity to improve people's homes and make customers happy	Must deal with all kinds of people, even the unfriendly and difficult ones
Jobs and tasks are varied	Some jobs are monotonous and dirty
No boss or coworkers to worry about	Must be able to work alone
Can set your own goals	Must review goals regularly and ensure they are reached to enjoy success

Handymen and women are often part-timers. The handyman business is often a great fit for retirees who are too young to stop working entirely, but who don't want the nine-to-five grind any longer. As a part-time business it also works well for anyone caring for other family members, be they children or elderly parents, and who wants or needs to work part time outside the home.

But the handyman business can also be an extremely lucrative full-time job. Let's look at the two options.

4.1 Part time

Running a part-time handyman business, and by that we mean less than about 30 hours per week, can work very well if you have other responsibilities that just don't allow you to work full-time hours. You may choose to work two or three days a week, or you may choose to work only when your time allows (e.g., when your spouse is on shift, or when the children are in school). Whatever works for you, you can be successful if you consider yourself — and sell yourself — as a professional.

Working part time can work well if you have other responsibilities that just don't allow you to work full-time hours.

Time management becomes a challenge if you choose the part-time option. As a handyman you are likely to run into jobs that will require long hours to complete and that must be done in one session. For example, a customer might need a staircase painted, and won't appreciate your disrupting the home by taking three days to complete an eight-hour job. Any jobs that require the power or water supply being turned off are other obvious cases when your schedule should not overly inconvenience your customer. If you choose to work part time, consider carefully how you will meet this kind of challenge and be clear about your schedule up front. One solution might be to team up with another part-time handyman and share some of the jobs, expenses and, of course profits.

As a part-time handyman, you will need to invest in the same amount of money and energy in starting and developing your business as a full-timer. You will need the same inventory of tools and equipment for completing jobs, a vehicle to get you around, and home headquarters in which to keep your records. A part-timer will likely get the same variety of jobs and will need a similar wide range of skills and abilities as a full-timer. Finally, marketing your business will require the same kind of attention and care as a full-time business.

4.2 Full time

Full-time handymen and women are professional and their work should show it. As with those who choose to work part time, a real commitment must be made by full-timers not only to working for customers as they hire you, but in managing your business.

Working full time means that you can realize the full potential of your business. You can make a very good wage if you can manage your customers and your business. Full time means scheduling work for yourself, 30 to 45 or more hours per week. Some weeks will be lighter and others will be heavier, but on average you can expect full-time hours and a full-time income.

Scheduling has its own challenges for those with a full time commitment. You must be accurate with your estimates of how long a job will take. You must also be able to let customers know that if they have additional work they want you to do once you are on site, you may or may not be able to squeeze it in.

Full-time handymen often have a tendency to never take a day off, a vacation, or even a statutory holiday! As a self-employed person, it's always tempting to work that one extra hour or day for the extra income, or because you're not sure when the next job will be offered to you. But be aware, for the sake of your business and your personal health, working full time does not mean all the time.

How you handle your schedule is up to you and your situation and goals. Consider carefully; if you don't give your needs the consideration they deserve, you will not be happy in your job, nor are you likely to be successful.

Chapter 2

GETTING STARTED

1. Your Goals and Expectations

Whenever you start a new venture or project, it is important to evaluate your expectations and assign realistic goals. By organizing your thoughts and making written goals, you will improve the chances for success tenfold. This chapter explores how to establish and achieve your business goals to set you on the road to success.

People often avoid goal-setting and tumble through life quite adequately. That is a luxury you cannot afford when starting your own business. Tumbling through life may be fine; tumbling through a business could spell disaster.

Think seriously about what you want from your business, both from a personal and a financial perspective. Do you want to work two days a week and make a little extra spending money, or seven days a week and make a fortune? It's up to you. Just remember, you won't get anywhere if you don't know where you're going.

Your business success is only limited by what you can envision and make happen.

If you are interested in starting a new handyman business, your first goal is to research the market and prepare for start-up. If you have already put your toe in the handyman waters, you may be looking to expand or professionalize your current business, in which case your goals may include identifying what works and what doesn't in your current set-up. You might need to think about investing in training, equipment, or advertising to meet your goals.

Before you go any further, ask yourself these questions:

- Why are you reading this book?
- What goals do you have for your business?
- What do you want your business to look like in two, five, or ten years?
- How will you know when you have accomplished your goals? (That is, what will be your measure of success?)

To answer these questions, write down your goals and the interim objectives needed to reach them. Be as specific as possible. Keep in mind that goals can, at times, be moving targets and that adjustments in timing are inescapable. Just try to keep your eye fixed on your target and make whatever corrections are necessary. Your business success is only limited by what you can envision and make happen. Having a clear vision of what you want from your business will allow you to recognize opportunities for success.

2. Sizing Up the Market

Whatever goals you have set for yourself, however modest, will be difficult to achieve if you do not have a good idea of the market and competition. Do you know if there are enough customers out there waiting to call you for their next home repair? How will you reach them? You need to take the time to answer these questions before you invest time in start-up planning and money in setting up shop, buying equipment, and hiring any professionals.

2.1 Market size

Your market is that segment of the population that potentially may use your handyman service. You may simply assume that your market is every homeowner who lives within a 50-mile radius of you, for example. But it may not be that simple. Yes, all homes need repair from time to time, but will the homeowners look to an outside service for help? For example, younger homeowners may try to do more work on their own because they don't have as much disposable income. On the other hand, two-income households may be more than happy to pass on jobs to a handyman because their time is limited. If your area has many condominium homes, the strata council may have arranged to have all repairs and renovations done by one or two larger businesses. Will this affect your market share?

To find out the size of your market, you need to do a little research. This is not as complicated as it may sound. Market research is simply the process of collecting and analyzing information. That information forms the basis for sound decision-making. It will help you pinpoint advertising and develop a marketing plan.

2.2 Market research

Market research can provide you with valuable information on who current and potential customers are, if there is a need for a handyman business in your area, and how you will measure up against the competition. By doing some market research on your own, you can prevent costly mistakes.

Start by looking in the local newspaper, which usually has ads for handyman services or contractors. These ads will give you some basic information on how many handyman services are advertising.

Open your eyes and ears to the information all around you. Ask your neighbors and acquaintances if they know of any handyman services in the area. Use the information you get to fine-tune your business plan. Don't let the fact that there is competition worry you! Find your niche by offering slightly different services, such as focusing on older homes, offering specialized seasonal services, or using only environmentally friendly products.

For more information about potential customers, check the demographic statistics to be sure your chosen market exists in large enough numbers to support your business. For example, if you have identified your customers as owners of older homes, or as single seniors or busy families, you need to determine how many of each category of customer exists in your proposed service area. Most public libraries have valuable information on the demographics of a given community, which is generally free and easy to access. The librarian can help you find the numbers you need.

Market research will help you pinpoint advertising and develop a marketing plan.

It is important to keep abreast with what your competitors are offering to customers.

If, after your research, you discover that the market you thought existed isn't large enough, you may have to adjust your business plan. Perhaps you need to broaden your market, service area, or areas of handyman specialization. Don't give up! Just be sure to enter the market with your eyes open and with a realistic picture of how much work is out there.

2.3 Facing the competition

You also want to know how competitive your market is. Will you be the only handyman service within a certain area, or are there several competitive services out there? Competition is not a deterrent to going into business, but it is wise to know who your competitors are and where they are located so that you stand on equal ground. By identifying your competition, you can then observe what they do right and what they do wrong, and learn from this.

To evaluate the competition for handyman services in your community, look again at the ads in the local paper in the home renovations or handyman sections. These ads will tell you what services different businesses offer, and what their special offerings are, such as 10 percent off for seniors, or free estimates. Some may even give you a hint about what they charge.

You can also look in the Yellow Pages for more information or contact the local Chamber of Commerce for a list of handyman businesses. You can even call some of these competitors and ask a few questions as if you were a customer. All this information is intended to help you define your business and set out a plan to be better than your competition.

The competition will change and your business will grow. It is therefore important to keep abreast with what your competitors are offering to customers. You will need to periodically survey the market and find out how you can best position your business for continued success.

3. Developing Your Business Plan

A business plan is a document that states the purpose of your business, including the range of services you will supply. It also includes the goals you have for your business, with measurable, definite outcomes. The business plan is one of the most effective management tools a business can employ, and it can help keep you on track over several months and even years.

Sample 1 illustrates a modest business plan with goals, actions, time frame, and measure of success included for a basic tile-laying handyman business. You can create a similar plan for your business.

This simple format can be adapted and expanded as necessary for your business, no matter how large or small.

A more formal business plan will be necessary if you need to borrow money to start up your business. A bank or other financial institution will want to see a business plan that includes information on the assets and/or capital you already have, the amount of loan you need, how long you'll need to pay back the loan, and the purpose of the loan. If you must write a more formal business plan, use Checklist 1 to guide you through the process. Before you begin, ask your financial institution if any other information, or a specific format for the plan, is required.

If you need to borrow money to start up your business, a formal business plan will be necessary.

4. Business and Legal Requirements

Legal and business requirements vary by state and province. For current and accurate information, you need to check on the requirements for small businesses in your area. Start with your municipal government; ask for any information on rules pertaining to small-business start-ups. From there you can check into any state or provincial regulations, or even federal requirements you might need to meet. In the United States, contact your state tax office to find out what permits may be needed for sales tax. In Canada, with very few exceptions, businesses are obliged to collect and remit the goods and services tax (GST). Canadians can contact their local Canada Revenue Agency office for details on tax and filing requirements.

Sales tax is just one area you need to look into to ensure your business meets all legal requirements. There are a number of other areas you must consider.

4.1 Zoning and licensing

Almost all handyman businesses are home-based businesses. You need to make sure you are legally allowed to operate your business from your home where you live. Even though most of your work

BUSINESS PLAN FOR GOALS AND MEASURABLES

Goal	Actions	Time frame	Measure of success
Develop a client list	1. Collect all client names from the past and call them to verify information and tell them about my business. 2. Spread the word about my services to neighbors, friends, and acquaintances and add them to the list. 3. Post business cards at the mall and the do-it-yourself store.	Six months	List of 30 active clients
Develop skills for laying tile	1. Research courses available and enroll. 2. Contact tile layer and ask if I can help with a few jobs to learn. 3. Tile the hall floor at my house.	One year	Confident to take on tile jobs for clients. Take on two tile jobs in the next year.
Organize vehicle	1. List items needed in the vehicle. 2. Remove all items and clean interior. 3. Organize bins of tools and materials.	One month	By the end of next month, the vehicle is completely organized with a plan to keep it that way.

CHECKLIST 1
BUSINESS PLAN OUTLINE

Business name and contact information

Purpose of business

- ❏ Include services you will provide and to whom.
- ❏ List goals and measurables for your business.
- ❏ Explain the purpose of the business plan (e.g., need for a loan).

Business information

- ❏ Personal financial information (You may need to include tax returns and a credit report.)
- ❏ Business description (Include all the good characteristics that will help you succeed.)
- ❏ Business history (if there is one)

Personnel and organization

- ❏ Describe the legal business organization (i.e., sole proprietorship, partnership, or other).
- ❏ State how the work will be accomplished and by whom.

Marketing analysis

- ❏ Who will you market your services to?
- ❏ Is there competition? How will you compete and be successful?
- ❏ Include any research you have done regarding trends and need for your services.
- ❏ How will you market your business? (e.g., newspaper ads, word of mouth, flyers)
- ❏ Do you have any unique customer service strategies?
- ❏ How will you price your services?

Financial information

- ❏ If you need a loan, explain how the loan will be used.
- ❏ Include information on start-up costs for your business.
- ❏ Include a current balance sheet if you have one.
- ❏ Revenue versus costs: List expenses against your income. Analyze how much you need to make to cover your costs.

Financial projections

- ❏ Explain how you see your business growing. Will you hire a helper, expand your services?
- ❏ What are the financial goals of your business in the next year? In five years?

Appendixes

- ❏ Include a résumé and any other applicable information.

will be away from your home, you will likely have some kind of home office and workshop. Check zoning regulations before you start your business.

You also must be licensed to operate a business, or at least registered with the government. What licenses you need will vary among regions. In some areas, a locally obtained business license is all you need to get started. In others, federal and state or provincial licenses are required as well.

The cost of a business license is minimal. The penalty for operating without a license varies with the issuing local government.

4.2 Form of business

A business can be formed as a sole proprietorship, a partnership, or a limited company. A handyman business lends itself well to the sole proprietorship form of business. The sole proprietor is responsible for the business in its entirety. Debts that are incurred by the business are debts of the sole proprietor, as are the assets. There are many advantages to sole proprietorship, including low start-up costs, as well as the most freedom from regulation of all business forms. These may be important considerations, especially if you plan to start a part-time business and don't want to get bogged down by paperwork.

A partnership can work well if you plan to run your business with someone else. Like a sole proprietorship, a partnership has low start-up costs. As well, there may be tax advantages. However, a partnership must be registered, and it is essential to draw up a partnership agreement stipulating the responsibilities of each partner. You should consult with a lawyer if you want to create a partnership agreement.

If your business grows to the extent that you want the formal legal structure of incorporation as a limited company, you should seek tax and legal advice to weigh the advantages against the disadvantages.

4.3 Insurance

As a handyman you need additional insurance to your standard homeowner insurance. It is important to talk to a professional about your needs. If you start a business from your home without the proper insurance, you take the chance that it will void your existing coverage.

As an employer, you must also consider worker's compensation insurance. All the states in the us and all the provinces in Canada have specific requirements for providing insurance for injured workers. As an independent operator, you can also arrange worker's compensation for yourself. Check with your local government offices for specific advice on registering for worker's compensation and how to manage insurance claims.

Here are a few items you should discuss with an insurance professional:

- Insurance for your work vehicle with special consideration of a replacement vehicle should yours be unusable for a time

- Adequate insurance for your tools and other supplies in case of damage, theft, etc.

- Liability insurance to offset the cost of any damages caused by your business

- Disability insurance if you are injured and can no longer work

Take care of your insurance needs and review them periodically. Once you have your insurance plan in place, you can relax and get on with your real job as a handyman.

Your business will need a name that helps customers remember who you are and what you do.

4.4 Naming your business

Your business will need a name that helps customers remember who you are and what you do. The only rule of thumb to follow when choosing a name is to keep it simple. Take some time to brainstorm names; you might include family and friends in this task to broaden your choices. List every name you can think of that appeals to you. As you assess the competition, you'll see names of other companies that may inspire you.

Before you register your company name and certainly before you have any flyers, business cards, or other stationery printed, check to make sure you have a unique name that no one else in your area uses. You want to stand out from the crowd with a business name that will be associated with you alone. In the United States, your city or county clerk will tell you if the name you have chosen

is available for use. In Canada, a name search can be done through the provincial ministry that handles incorporations.

When you have chosen a name for your business, you should protect it by filing, or registering, the name with the appropriate authorities. Your name will be checked against previously filed names to ensure that it has not been taken by another business. Once your name is on file, it cannot be used by anyone else in that district.

4.5 Hiring employees or contract staff

If your business grows to the point where you need help, you will have to decide whether you want to hire an employee or perhaps hire occasional contract workers.

Becoming an employer requires you to assume a number of additional responsibilities as a business owner. You will have to register with the local labor authority, make arrangements to pay your employees on a regular basis, make the necessary tax payments to the government on behalf of your employees, maintain employee records, provide a safe work environment, provide training and supervision, supply and maintain the tools needed by your employees, and, most importantly, take legal and financial responsibility for your employees' actions.

Employer-employee rules and regulations are governed by the laws of the jurisdiction in which you live. If you want to hire an employee, you will need to conform to the law in terms of hours of work, minimum wage, workers compensation board coverage, vacation pay, severance pay, and so on. All this adds another management facet to your business and can take a substantial amount of time and effort. However, if you need to expand your operation and take on larger and more complicated jobs on a regular basis, this will be time and effort well spent.

If you need extra help on an occasional basis only, it is much more convenient to hire someone on a contract basis. This saves you the time and extra paperwork of having a regular employee. For most small handyman businesses, hiring contractors from time to time is probably the most practical solution. Unless your business grows significantly, it is unlikely you will be able to provide enough work to someone on a regular part-time or full-time basis.

In our business, we do not employ anyone full time, but we occasionally hire a student to assist with large summer jobs on a

Becoming an employer requires you to assume a number of additional responsibilities as a business owner.

contract basis. We pay more than the minimum wage and supply all the necessary tools and equipment. We have opted to keep our handyman business small and easy to manage. When necessary, Kevin can also call on other tradespeople he knows to complete portions of work on contract to the customer.

5. Accounting Basics

Every business must keep accurate and thorough financial records covering all income received and expenses incurred. Records help you produce income, control expenses, plan growth and cash flow, keep tax payments to a minimum, and comply with the multitude of regulations.

5.1 Bookkeeping

If you keep your accounting system simple, you'll be much more likely to use it. Your first step is to open a business bank account. Make sure you get a deposit book for recording your deposits and some business checks for making business purchases. Each month when your bank statement arrives you can do a bank reconciliation to give you a clear picture of what you have earned. It is important to keep these deposits and records separate from your personal bank account.

As you start up, you may wish to hire an accountant or book-keeper to design a system for recording the information for your particular circumstances. If you are confident enough to set up your own system, you may want to purchase one of the many available accounting software programs to help you keep accurate records. Accounting software provides a general ledger, accounts receivable, accounts payable, and invoicing functions. It will also print monthly statements for all your accounts. A good accounting package will tell you who owes money, how much they owe, and if the payment is overdue and by how many days. The invoicing portion of such programs usually provides a professional-looking bill for presentation to your customer.

5.2 Your balance sheet

A balance sheet is a useful tool that gives a snapshot of the financial condition of your business at any given point in time. A balance sheet includes assets, liabilities, and owner's equity. An asset is anything

You must keep accurate financial records.

the business owns that has monetary value. Liabilities are debts the business owes to creditors. To keep track of the value of your business, you should routinely complete a balance sheet to help you understand where your money goes and what you have invested in your business's assets. Again, a good accounting software package will help you print out regular balance sheets. See Sample 2 for an example of a typical balance sheet. In a small home-based business, some of the categories shown in this example may not apply; you can adapt your balance sheet to suit your own business.

5.3 Tax requirements

You must keep accurate financial records of all your business expenses and receipts for taxation purposes. With these records, you can legally deduct all of the relevant home-business expenses on your income tax. In most areas, you can deduct any business-use-of home expenses, those expenses associated with maintaining a work space in your home. These can include a portion of many of your home expenses including heat, electricity, and insurance. You can calculate how much you can deduct by figuring out what proportion of your home you use for your business, and then using that number to deduct the expenses. For example, if you use 200 square feet of a 1,000-square foot home for business, this constitutes 20 percent of the total space. You can therefore deduct 20 percent of all your home-related expenses. Tools, supplies, and other materials you use to conduct your business can also be deducted as business expenses. Receipts for your business purchases add up and make a significant difference. So make sure you keep all your receipts and remember that they are required to back up your tax claim.

6. Getting Professional Help for Your Business

Running a successful business of any kind takes a team. Your business is no different. When you encounter an area of your business where you need help, consider hiring outside experts. For example, you may want to hire an accountant to prepare your taxes. A professional organizer can help you set up your home headquarters, your filing system, or your storage space. There are specialists available to help with marketing and business planning as well. And, of course, whenever legal advice is needed, you should seek the services of a lawyer.

BALANCE SHEET

HANDYMAN UNLIMITED

Statement of Assets and Liabilities as of [date] _____

ASSETS

CURRENT ASSETS
Cash _____
Accounts receivable _____
Inventory _____
Prepaid expenses _____
Other current assets _____
Total current assets $_____

FIXED ASSETS
Land and buildings (net) _____
Equipment (net) _____
Other fixed assets _____
Total fixed assets $_____

OTHER ASSETS
Other assets _____
Total other assets $_____

Total assets $_____

LIABILITIES AND EQUITY

CURRENT LIABILITIES
Accounts payable _____
Taxes payable _____
Other current liabilities _____
Total current liabilities $_____

LONG-TERM LIABILITIES
Long-term loans payable _____
Other long-term liabilities _____
Total long-term liabilities $_____

EQUITY
Net equity _____
Retained earnings _____
Total equity $_____

Total liabilities and equity $_____

If you already have contacts in these various fields, give them a call and ask for an appointment to discuss your needs as you begin your new business. If you do not currently have contacts in any one of these areas, ask friends, family, and even neighbors for referrals. The relationship you have with these professionals is important and you need to have faith in their advice. Word of mouth is often the best way to make contact. You may want to get a number of quotes from various professionals before making a choice. Be up front and let the professional know you are shopping around for services, and give them a chance to explain what they can offer.

You should also seek expert help in any area of your handyman work where your own safety or that of the homeowner is at stake. For example, it may be okay to do simple electrical work, such as replacing a light fixture or moving a plug, as long as you are comfortable and confident that you can do it with no risk. But if you run into a task that is unfamiliar, you should turn to a licensed tradesperson for advice. You may even want to hire a licensed tradesperson for some aspects of your business. (For more on developing a network of tradespeople, see Chapter 4.)

Many communities have home-business network groups. Ask about these in your area and join one if you can. Network groups can offer a wealth of contacts and information as your business grows.

Chapter 3

SETTING UP SHOP

1. Getting Organized

No matter how small or large you plan your business to be, you need to be well organized. For the handyman, this means carving out a work space to serve as your office, equipping and maintaining a vehicle that will be your office on the road, and building an inventory of tools and supplies to always have on hand, ready to be put to work at your next job.

It pays to take the time to get organized before you become very busy with your new business venture. If you pile up the paperwork on the front seat of your truck, neglect to file invoices and bills in an organized fashion, and put off all the administrative work for another day, you may soon find yourself overwhelmed. For example, when customers ask you to fax them a price quote, will your office fax be up and running? Or will you still be thinking about getting around to setting up your systems? If you do not have the right tools and supplies to do a job when requested, will the customer

Your business space should be located where you can work without distractions.

wait for you? Or will the job be given to someone else? Being organized can make all the difference between business success and failure.

2. Your Home Headquarters

Many handymen make the mistake of thinking that if they can do the work and keep their customers happy, that's all they have to do to run a successful business. Not true. Every business needs to be managed if it is to provide a living, grow, achieve goals, and ultimately be successful according to its particular needs.

One of the benefits of running a handyman business is that you don't have to invest in expensive retail or other office space. You do, however, need to have some sort of headquarters where you can take care of the business side of your job. As long as you have some room in your home and some space to store supplies, you can be organized and set up to start your business in short order.

Your business headquarters may be a spare room in your house, a corner of your garage, or even the dining room table, as long as it is somewhere you can a organize your files and important records, and do paperwork such as invoicing, quoting, and bookkeeping. You may need some additional space to store tools and equipment, but that can be separate from your office area. Perhaps a corner of the garage or the basement would be suitable.

You want your business space to be somewhere you can work without distractions, a place where you can leave work and come back to it undisturbed, a place where you can concentrate. It can be anywhere and any size, as long as it accommodates your need to —

- ⚒ create, store, and retrieve information and records;
- ⚒ communicate with customers and other contacts; and
- ⚒ work on your business in relative comfort.

Let's first look at each of these requirements in turn, and then focus on the special considerations of a home office: the tax advantages and the challenges of keeping your home and business separate.

2.1 Keeping records

Whether you use a computer or an old-fashioned paper filing system, you need to maintain records in order to stay organized and keep your business running smoothly. You will need to create and organize the following files:

- *Customer files.* A complete record of your customers is vital and should include names, addresses, phone numbers, e-mail addresses (if using), work done, and work that needs to be done. These should be kept up-to-date and easily available. With customers' contact information readily at hand, you can return phone calls promptly, set up appointments, or follow up in any way.

- *Contact files.* It is useful to have files for every business contact, such as tradespeople you can call on to help complete a job, accountant, lawyer, and insurance agent. Each file should contain all contact information, as well as any contracts/policy numbers and so on. If this information is not readily available when you need it, you may waste valuable time looking for it — time that could be better spent working for customers.

- *Accounting tax files.* Several files are needed to keep your bookkeeping in order — for outstanding customer invoices, bills to be paid, office expenses, and so on. Keep in mind that you must carefully track your business expenses and keep all receipts so you can use them as deductions at tax time.

- *Tax files.* Separate from your accounting files, a tax file is also a good idea. Here you can keep your tax returns, any current information on taxation and small business, and any correspondence from the tax department.

- *Inventory files.* Because tools are such a key part of the handyman business, it is important to keep careful track of them. An up-to-date list of all the tools and equipment you own for your business, including warranties, is essential. If you are storing your equipment and supplies in different places, it is also useful to record where everything is kept. Use Worksheet 2 to keep track of your tools.

- *Marketing and general business files.* Here you might include any business and marketing information you have created such as business cards, letterhead, advertisements, flyers, news articles, and so on.

WORKSHEET 2
TOOLS AND MATERIALS INVENTORY

Location	Item	Make and model	Serial number	Original cost	Replacement cost
				Totals	

To keep all these files organized, you will need some sort of filing cabinet. If you are using a computer filing system, you still need a storage area for paper, warranties, receipts, and so on. Take the time to buy a few file folders and label them according to your needs. Get into the habit early of filing paperwork as soon as it comes in. If you leave it lying around on the table or desk for a few days, it is likely to get misplaced and not be available when you need it. Here are a few organizational tips:

Get into the habit of filing paperwork as soon as you receive it.

- Have a place to file all items you deal with in your work and put everything back when you're finished with it.

- Use large brown envelopes labeled with the customers' names to collect and keep receipts as they come in, if you need to track expenses for several different customers at one time.

- Allot some time each week to organize and reorganize your files. Doing this regularly is time well spent as it avoids wasting valuable time searching for something.

- Organize each day. Arrange the tools and equipment required for each job, organize the items you need to return to the hardware store, call a vendor about a replacement part, and so on.

- Keep it simple. The less complicated your organization method is, the more likely you will be to maintain it.

2.2 Communication needs

How are you going to communicate with your customers? How will you prepare quotes, invoices, and marketing material for your business? Even though most of your business will be conducted outside the home office, you need to have some method of staying in touch with your customers and other contacts. Here are some items to consider:

- *Telephone.* Ideally, you will arrange to have a telephone line separate from your home line. Some handymen manage to run successful businesses without paying the extra cost for a business line, but if you choose this route, both you and your family must be very disciplined. Will your children know how to take messages and answer the phone in a professional way? Do you have teenagers who frequently tie up the phone line, leaving potential customers frustrated when they can't get through? For the few extra dollars a month, it is well worth installing a phone line dedicated to your business. This will also help your advertising, because you can list your business phone number in the telephone book under your business's name. Having a business phone is also a clear indication to the tax department that you are in a credible business and that all those deductions you are claiming are legitimate. (See section **2.4** for information on tax advantages.)

⌇ *Answering machine/service.* Whether you have a separate business phone line or your home and business phone lines are shared, you must have a suitable phone message to greet prospective customers. Make sure your message is polite, professional, and clear. It should state the name of your business and ask callers to leave a message including their name and return phone number.

⌇ *Cell phone.* You might consider purchasing a cell phone for your business. As the handyman business requires you to be away from your office most of the time, it is helpful to have a means for customers to contact you anytime, anywhere. In fact, one option may be to have a cell phone only for your business, rather than setting up a separate land line in your home office. That way you can answer the calls whenever you are available and let your voice mail take care of the rest.

⌇ *Computer.* A computer isn't essential, but it does help streamline much of the paperwork necessary to keep a small business operating smoothly. You can set up your customer contact files, do your bookkeeping, and even design and print your business cards and letterhead on computer. If you don't already have a home computer and don't want to incur the expense of buying one as you start up, you can certainly function without one. But remember that the cost of a computer for your business is tax deductible, and you may find that the time it saves you in the long run is well worth the investment.

⌇ *E-mail and Internet access.* E-mail has become the preferred method of communication for many people today. Some of your customers may want to receive information and quotes from you by e-mail; others won't. By having e-mail you offer your customers another option for communicating with you — and that means better customer service, which should translate into more work for you. The Internet can also be useful in many ways. For example, you can search the Internet for a hard-to-find tool or specialized information on a technique needed to finish a job. As your business grows, you might even want to create your own simple web page to advertise your services.

☞ *Fax.* Today, a fax machine is a necessity of business. Many of your customers will want quotes sent to them by fax, and you may find it useful to receive information from suppliers this way. If you can't immediately afford a fax machine, a mailbox or office service business can look after outgoing and incoming fax transmissions for a small fee. Most computers have fax software included in them that allows you to send electronic faxes — another reason to consider purchasing a computer for your business.

☞ *Printer.* Printers can be useful in conjunction with your computer. For example, you can print your own business cards and letterhead if you don't want to go to the expense of professionally designed and printed artwork. A relatively inexpensive printer will likely handle all your printing needs.

Your office area should be as functional and attractive as possible.

2.3 Your office environment

Once you have selected the area of your home to use for your business, do some planning. You want the space to be as functional and attractive as possible. With a little thought before you organize your space, you can increase the chances of achieving the results you want.

Make a list of the furniture, equipment, and supplies you need for your home office. Beside each item, note whether there are any special requirements. For example, if you are going to set up a computer, phone, and fax machine, make sure you have the appropriate power outlets. These are important planning steps; don't bypass them. You will be frustrated and annoyed if you discover later that you have not allowed enough space for a filing cabinet and desk or if you have misjudged your electrical requirements.

It is easy to underestimate the space required for storage and filing. In planning your office space, remember that you'll need somewhere to put everything associated with your business — stationery, office supplies, business records, and so on. You can separate stored items into two categories: those that need to be close by and those that don't. Your customer files should be close at hand, for example, but you don't need your tools beside your desk, and you probably don't need your longer-term files, such as tax information, nearby. If you have other space in your home, such as an empty linen closet or a corner of the basement, you can use it for those things you don't need to access on a daily basis. Set up bins for specific tasks such as painting or drywall repair. Label each bin and put all the tools and materials needed for these small jobs in the bins. You can then pick up a particular bin and go to the job without having to hunt around for the tools you need.

2.4 Tax advantages to the home office

Generally speaking, you are allowed to deduct that portion of your house used for business purposes if it is your principal place of business. Also, your home office must be used exclusively by the business to earn business income. For example, you cannot use a room for a bedroom at night and an office during the day.

The allowed deductions include rent, mortgage interest, heating, electricity, and other expenses in a ratio to the area of the house used for the business. A good idea is to take measurements of your working area. You can check with your accountant to be sure you are following the latest rules.

Your business phone and computer are also tax deductible. Keep a record of all long-distance charges and telephone extensions used for business purposes. For the computer, you can deduct the portion you use for your business. The tax department assumes that a home computer is used for both business and personal reasons, so you should keep a detailed record of your computer usage on a daily basis.

An important deduction for the handyman is a vehicle. Your business depends on using a car, van, or truck for getting to and from jobs, and you can therefore claim all vehicle expenses that relate to the business including gasoline, repairs and maintenance, insurance, and parking charges. Purchase a car expense logbook at any business stationery store and record all expenses, both business and personal. You can then calculate the business portion of your expenses by dividing the total miles driven in the year by the total business miles driven.

Other legitimate home business expenses that are tax deductible include the following:

- All licenses, dues, and subscriptions including business license and trade magazines

- All advertising costs, which includes any flyers your may print

- Any office expense from desk to paper clips, if it is intended for use in your operation. This includes computer supplies, file folders, rubber stamps, staplers, and any other small items that you need to organize and run your enterprise. It also includes larger items such as furniture and filing cabinets.

- Business cards, stationery, or any other special forms needed for your business

- All consultations with your lawyer and accountant. This includes preparation of your tax return.

- Courses to help you run your business or update your knowledge on a particular handyman trade or technique

2.5 Keeping your home and office separate

There are so many advantages to having a home office and being able to base your business out of a room in your house or apartment. But there are unique challenges to this arrangement as well, and these should be addressed early on.

You need to learn how to blend your family life with your business life without neglecting either. Having a well-organized home headquarters is a good first step. If your files, tools, and supplies are organized and stored away from the daily family area, you will find life much easier. It also helps to use a calendar to keep track of and coordinate family and business schedules. You will of course need some kind of planning calendar for your business appointments, but it will also help if you can see at a glance when you can or cannot take on jobs because of your family's schedule. A bulletin board is another useful aide for staying organized. On it you can tack papers, receipts, items for filing, customer keys (labeled, of course), and so on.

For a business to merge successfully with family life, you must be able to leave it behind. Some home-based business owners become almost obsessed with their operation and find it impossible to stop thinking or talking about it. Many find themselves doing

You need to learn to blend your family life with your business life without neglecting either.

paperwork and marketing in the evenings or late at night after a full day's work, and on weekends. For your family's sake, don't turn yourself into a home workaholic. This is another reason for establishing that separate, self-contained work space. Closing the door at the end of your workday gives you a clear dividing line between work and family needs.

3. Your Vehicle — An Office Away from Home

Since your vehicle will likely be a portable office, workshop, consultation room, lunchroom, and rest area, it needs to be appropriate to your purposes, reliable, and outfitted with what you need. It also must be properly insured for business use. Some insurance companies offer small business insurance packages that are a cost-effective way of meeting all your insurance requirements in one bundle. Typically, these bundles include property coverage and general liability coverage, along with vehicle coverage.

So what type of vehicle do you need? Consider the type of jobs you'll be taking on. If you will frequently be using lawnmowers, snowblowers, and other large equipment, you need a larger, heavier vehicle and/or trailer. If you plan on doing mostly painting, small repairs, and assembly-type work, you may get by with a smaller vehicle.

3.1 Van, truck, or car?

The most important consideration in your choice of business vehicle is having enough room to store your tools and materials. If your car is equipped with a good roof rack to transport equipment, then you may not need a larger vehicle. A removable roof rack will allow you to carry larger heavy loads, such as ladders and wood. However, you will notice a dramatic reduction in gas mileage if you use a small car for heavy loads, and the wear and tear on your vehicle can be significant.

If you must make do with a car for your business, you might consider hitching a small wagon to the back to haul more supplies and tools. Or you might be able to pick up a suitable vehicle second-hand. Some older-model station wagons make excellent handyman vehicles. If reliable, the larger engines, storage space, and roof area make them a good choice.

A van can be a good compromise for a vehicle that is going to be used for both work and family. The modern minivans are convenient because their seats are easily removed for storage. If you use large bins to store your tools and other supplies, you can easily transform the work van back to the family van as needed. Just remove the bins and add the seats. As well, a trailer can easily be hitched up to a van, and many vans also have built-in roof racks, adding even more storage and transport space. The gas mileage is reasonable in a minivan as are the costs of repairs and replacement parts.

Another option is a used utility van. If the van has been part of a fleet, it has probably been well looked after and has many years of life left in it. Often utility vans have built-in storage and roof racks, so they are perfect for a handyman business.

A truck is also an excellent option. A two-wheel drive, full-size pickup is fine for most work. It has the ability to take high loads in an open box, and it can usually handle very heavy loads as well. A four-wheel drive truck may be an excellent investment if you plan on doing snow plowing and/or heavy landscaping work. It all depends on your assessment of your needs.

Consider that passenger room is often limited in a pickup truck, so if you need room for helpers, a large cab may be in order. An eight-foot box is best for transporting sheets of drywall, plywood, lumber, and a cap will keep everything dry and safe.

Whatever vehicle you choose, make sure you can answer yes to the following questions:

- Does it meet your needs and the type of jobs you will take on?
- Is it reliable?
- Is it safe (for both passengers and for your tools and equipment)?
- Can you expect to cover the cost of operating the vehicle with your business income?

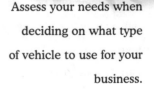

Assess your needs when deciding on what type of vehicle to use for your business.

3.2 Using trailers and wagons

A trailer or wagon can greatly expand your transportation options. You can use it only when you need it, which gives great flexibility with your chosen vehicle. There are many types of trailers on the

Your vehicle will be your office away from home, so you will need to equip it with certain items that you should always have on hand.

market from open top 4-foot x 6-foot models to covered workshops. Again, look at what you realistically need. We have a 4-foot x 7-foot homemade trailer that was given to Kevin by a customer. It was in sad shape and destined for the dump before some paint, a little welding, and some new wood brought it back to life. Now it serves a range of purposes, from hauling topsoil to delivering furniture to transporting junk to the dump. A trailer or wagon is a great investment and with a little TLC can be yours for life.

A single-axle trailer is a good option for the handyman who does a lot of lawn and yard work. Most come with open sides and a ramp, with a 1,500-lb. load capacity. The 4-foot x 8-foot or 5-foot x 8-foot sizes work well for most jobs and are very versatile and lightweight. In this size of trailer you can haul topsoil, shingles, bulky loads of drywall, lumber, and even a lawn tractor. Keep in mind what the load capacity is and do regular maintenance to make the trailer last a lifetime.

Covered trailers offer security and protection for their contents. At the end of the day you just load up and take your workshop with you, or lock it and leave it on-site. Most come in widths of 5 or 6 feet, with a length of 8 feet and a payload of 2,500 lbs. They are big enough to hold most supplies, tools, and other items. The price is higher, but in many cases the security and protection offered may be worth it if you don't have a lot of storage room in your home.

Whatever trailer you choose, have a trained person install the hitch and wire the lights for your vehicle. Safety is the first concern, so have a professional make sure the trailer is secure when being pulled, and that all the lights are operating.

Depending on where you live and how large your vehicle is, you may be required to have an annual safety inspection. You will also need to have your trailer licensed and you may need additional insurance. Check with your local licensing office for information.

3.3 Vehicle supplies

Because your vehicle will be your office away from home, you will need to equip it with certain items that you should always have on hand. This may mean that you duplicate some of your records (e.g., keep a customer/client list at home and in your vehicle). Other items will be useful to have readily available no matter what handyman job you take on.

Here's a list to help you get organized. You will want to add to it as you develop your on-the-job experience.

- First-aid kit
- Emergency kit including jumper cables, flares, and any other items for vehicle breakdowns
- Bottled water
- Insect repellant
- Sunscreen lotion
- Nonperishable snacks
- Work gloves
- Dust masks
- Safety goggles
- Calculator, pens, and paper
- Quote forms
- Reference books and information that may be needed on the job
- Customer contact forms (see Sample 9 in Chapter 4)
- Contact numbers
- Change of clothes including extra shoes and rubber boots
- Rags for cleanup
- Rope, 25 feet
- Plastic bags, large and small
- Garbage bags and heavy nylon bags for weighty items
- Flashlight and batteries
- Power cord, 25 feet
- Tarp, 12 feet x 12 feet

Just as you need to keep your home office organized, you should strive to keep your vehicle organized. Line the floor of your van or truck with old carpet or a drop cloth to avoid paint disasters. Keep maps and important phone numbers on hand. Use small storage containers to keep the items listed above in order and in place.

4. Tools — The Handyman's Best Friend

The biggest investment in your handyman business may well be your tools. You need many different tools for the many different jobs you will take on, and good-quality, reliable tools will help you do the job right. In starting out, and as you develop your business, consider carefully what tools you need in order to meet your customers' specific needs.

To keep your tools in good working order, you must store and maintain them properly. For example, if you keep a handsaw in a bin with other metal tools, it will soon become dull and useless. Be sure to keep guards on sharp tools to avoid injuries. Schedule time to clean, oil, and generally maintain your tools regularly.

Your tools can be a business tax write-off, so keep all your tool receipts filed with your other expenses. File warranties and instructions carefully and add new items to your inventory (see Worksheet 2).

4.1 A basic tool kit

If you are seriously considering running a handyman business, you probably have many tools already. Use the following list to fill the gaps in your existing supply and to build your basic tool kit. You may not need all of these tools, depending on the type of work you will do.

- Paint brush and rollers
- Roller pole
- Paint tray and two liners
- Masking, electrical, and duct tape
- Measuring tape, 25 feet or more
- Claw hammer
- Screwdrivers
- Nails and assorted screws
- Sandpaper
- Power tester
- Angle square
- Cordless drill with attachable bits

Your tools can be a business tax write-off, so keep all your tool receipts filed with your other expenses.

- Palm sander
- Handsaw
- Hacksaw
- Chalk line and chalk
- Small level
- Set of Allen keys
- Pry bar
- Staple gun and staples
- Stud finder
- Locking pliers
- Wire cutters
- Yard tools
- Wood filler
- Wood glue
- Paint scraper
- Putty knife
- Spray oil
- Needle-nose pliers
- Adjustable wrench and wrench set (standard and metric)

Of course, there are other "nice to have" items. Often having specialized tools will make the job go more smoothly and quickly, so you might consider some of these tools to add to your basic kit:

- Drywall hammer and square
- Long and stubby set of screwdrivers
- Power tools such as a jigsaw, belt sander, biscuit joiner, skill saw, and reciprocating saw
- Respirator
- Crowbar
- Portable workbench
- Clamps

Renting tools can be very cost effective.

⚒ Heavy-duty shop vac

⚒ Laser level

⚒ Sledgehammer

One of the best investments we have made is a compressor and a set of air tools. They are fast, clean, and easy to use on a wide variety of projects. Depending on the size of compressor, the cost can be reasonable and you can expect a long life out of the tools if you do routine maintenance.

4.2 The right tools for the job

It is not feasible to have on hand every tool you will ever need. Jobs are all unique, materials change, and it just doesn't make sense to buy tools that you'll need only once or twice in your career. It can be very expensive to keep buying tools in this way, even if you do get a tax write-off. Cost is one thing, but storage is another important consideration. Unless you have an abundance of space, the storing of tools can become a problem. Some tools, such as the ones in the basic toolkit, will pay for themselves many times over, so it's wise to buy the best quality possible on those items. For other items you may need only occasionally, you should consider renting, buying at a reduced price, or borrowing.

Renting tools and equipment can be very cost effective. For example, we sometimes need to rent a scaffold or a floor sander to complete a job. Renting is convenient and the cost can be directly covered in the bill to your customer. Here are some tips on renting tools:

⚒ Research rental companies in your area to find out what they have.

⚒ Get price lists and keep them on hand to help in estimating costs for the customer.

⚒ Include rental company information in your network contact file for easy reference.

⚒ Build a relationship with your favored rental company; they'll get to know you and may give you a better deal.

⚒ Ask questions about what you have rented and find out how to use it so that you work safely and efficiently.

Buying tools and supplies at a reduced price is obviously a good way to expand your variety of tools and therefore the types of jobs you can take on. Local hardware stores often have tool sales, and sometimes you can find warehouse or factory sales. Watch out that what you are buying is in good condition and comes with all the pieces. Some sales are on reconditioned items that may not be as good value as they first appear.

Secondhand stores are also a source for used and reconditioned tools. However, be aware that contractors often dump old, worn-out tools and equipment in these stores. Make sure you test and thoroughly check whatever you are buying.

Garage sales can also be a fruitful source for buying tools. Small hand tools, collections of old hardware, and yard tools can often be found for a fraction of the price of buying new.

Here are some tips on tool buying:

- Buy the best you can afford for your basic toolkit.
- Always check out the condition and test reduced price and secondhand tools.
- Read instructions and maintenance suggestions.
- File your warranties and receipts.

Borrowing tools is another option if you need something specific for a short period of time. Ask your network of contacts if they can lend you the tool. Just be prepared to do the same for someone else when the time comes. You may also ask if your customer has the item you need. Many people have tools and equipment but don't use them, and they may have just what you need for the job.

Chapter 4

MARKETING YOUR BUSINESS

It's time to get the word out. You're organized, enthusiastic, and ready to go, but now you need to find those all-important first customers. How do you reach them? And once your business gets off the ground and you start working regularly, how do you keep all the jobs scheduled and on track?

1. Letterhead and Business Cards

If you want people to know you're in business, you have to look like you're in business. That means you need business cards to hand out when you talk to people, and letterhead prepared for when you are asked for estimates and quotes on jobs.

Your business card may be the first contact a potential customer has with your business. It should be professional and establish an identity that accurately represents you and your expertise. Office software makes the production of personalized letterhead, business cards, and invoices inexpensive and quick. Alternatively, having your stationery made by an outside source need not be expensive. Keep the design simple and clear. Remember that the idea is to communicate what you do in a way that encourages customers to call you.

Sample 3 shows a simple business card with a tag line. You can add more information to your business card if you wish, including your address, cell phone number, and perhaps a simple logo.

Word of mouth is very important to a handyman business.

SAMPLE 3
BUSINESS CARD

HANDYMAN UNLIMITED

Call Kevin

905-555-0055

NO JOB TOO ODD!

Once you have your business cards in hand, give them to friends, neighbors, and family members. Ask them to tell everyone they know about the services you offer. If you are starting your business from scratch, you'll need to find a few customers to get you started. Spread the word that your handyman business is open. You will probably start with small jobs and work up from there. At every job, leave your business card behind.

2. Word of Mouth

The handyman business is particularly affected by word of mouth. Because handyman jobs are short term and often small in nature, people don't seem to want to spend a lot of time interviewing potential contractors and hunting down someone the way they might for larger, long-term jobs. Often, customers are in a hurry to get the work done, and they want to find someone who can do the job well as soon as possible. They will therefore often ask friends and neighbors for referrals.

If you have already done a few odd jobs around the neighborhood, and your customers have been pleased with your work, they will likely tell others. But keep in mind you still have to advertise your services and create your own word of mouth advertising. For example, when Kevin works at a customer's house, perhaps doing yard work or painting, and is asked if he knows someone who can fix the roof, his answer is, "Yes, I can!"

3. Advertising

Because word of mouth and client referrals are so important to the handyman business, you don't need to go overboard with formal advertising for your business. However, a few simple flyers distributed throughout the neighborhood or posted on community bulletin boards or at the local hardware store may help to bring in customers.

Simple flyers need not be expensive. If you have some basic software on your computer and a good-quality printer, you can design and print your flyers in the comfort of your home office. Be sure to include the following information:

- Who you are (your business name)
- What services you offer
- How your services can solve customers' problems
- How to contact you

Samples 4 and 5 illustrate the kind of simple flyer you can easily design on your own. Sample 6 is a seasonal reminder that you can distribute when the busy summer work season is winding down.

If you are prepared to spend a little extra, you could consider putting a small ad in the Yellow Pages of your local telephone directory, or perhaps in your community newspaper. People often turn to these sources for handyman help.

Samples 7 and 8 illustrate simple ads that could be used in the Yellow Pages or in local newspapers.

4. Build on Existing Clients

Once you have developed a roster of satisfied clients, build on that resource. It's a wasted opportunity to walk away from a completed job and never contact that customer again. Use the Customer Contact Form shown in Sample 9 to keep track of every customer and note what other work might be done for them. After you have

NEED A HANDYMAN?

NO JOB TOO BIG OR SMALL.
CALL FOR A FREE ESTIMATE.

Kevin 905-555-0005

HANDYMAN UNLIMITED

- Assemble everything from barbecues to bikes
- Paint, plaster, and polish
- Remove rubbish
- Yard work and cleanup
- Local, friendly, and honest

CALL HANDYMAN UNLIMITED!
I CAN HELP.

Kevin 905-555-0005

The Fall is coming!!!

Do you need help with —

- Yard cleanup
- Outside maintenance
- Weatherproofing your home
- Hanging holiday decorations
- Winterizing your sunroom
- Any other job around the house

CALL HANDYMAN UNLIMITED.

Quality Work Guaranteed. Thanks for your business!

Kevin 905-555-0005

SAMPLE 7
YELLOW PAGES ADVERTISEMENT

NEED A HANDYMAN?

- Painting
- Decks
- Small jobs

Best prices/honest work

Call Kevin Pegg
905-555-0005

finished a job and a few days or weeks have gone by, call your customer and make sure they are satisfied. At that time ask if there is any other job you can perform for them. Many customers will ask if you can do a job later, perhaps next season. In this case, don't wait for them to call you; follow up at the appropriate time.

It is also helpful to ask your customers if they know anyone else who might benefit from your service. If you get leads — names of companies or individuals who might hire you — drop off a flyer and follow up with a telephone call to introduce yourself.

You can also develop a more personalized note or flyer to leave with your customers at the end of a job. This type of flyer provides you with an opportunity to advertise other types of jobs you can do. Samples 10 and 11 illustrate two options for this type of flyer. Again, don't forget to follow up!

5. Networking

For the handyman, networking has two aspects. First, as discussed previously, you want to continue to build your network of customer contacts by handing out business cards and asking for client referrals. You also want to network, where possible, if you participate in any short courses to learn a new skill, attend trade shows, or join a

CUSTOMER CONTACT FORM

Customer Contact Form

Name:		Dates of contact:
Address:		
Phone:		
E-mail:		

Notes on work performed:

Work to call about in the future:

Special notes and precautions:

Thanks for your business!

If you need my services again in the future, please give me a call.

As we discussed, there are some rotten boards in your fence. I could come in the spring to replace them. I estimate the cost at about $300. Also, you mentioned that you'd like to have your dining room painted. I do painting and would be happy to discuss an estimate with you; just give me a call. Thanks again for everything and have a great summer.

Kevin

Call Kevin: 905-555-0005
HANDYMAN UNLIMITED

HANDYMAN UNLIMITED

CUSTOMER FOLLOW-UP NOTE (2)

Thanks for choosing **HANDYMAN UNLIMITED!** The work you requested has been done and I have noted a few areas where some further work may be needed around your home. Please give me a call if you would like a free estimate or more information. I offer seasonal services at a special rate.

_____
_____
_____
_____
_____

HANDYMAN UNLIMITED
Call any time. Kevin: 905-555-0005

Here are a few of the other services I provide:

- Assembly of products and furniture
- Help with moving
- Junk removal
- Yard cleanup
- Basement and shed cleanup
- Grass cutting and weeding
- Snow removal
- House painting, inside and out
- Furniture refinishing and repair
- Small engine tune-ups
- Tile floors
- Kitchen counters
- Bathroom renovations
- Decks and patios
- Small additions
- Window replacement
- Minor electrical jobs
- Delivery of items

HANDYMAN UNLIMITED

Always keep a supply of business cards on hand.

small business organization. Always keep a supply of business cards on hand and don't be shy about introducing yourself and offering your services.

The other aspect of networking is building on your list of contacts in other trades. As discussed in Chapter 2, you will want to establish a network of people you can call on to help you complete a job, ask advice, and get prices, references, and other information. Your list will grow over time, and these people provide yet another opportunity for finding new customers. As your contacts become familiar with your business and work standards, they are likely to willingly pass on your name to potential customers. They may even call on you to help them with some of their jobs.

You can use a Network Contact Form (see Sample 12), similar to the Customer Contact Form, to help you keep track of your contacts. You should develop and list contacts in the following trades and areas:

- Plumbers
- Electricians
- Carpenters
- Tile layers
- Stonemasons
- Arborists
- Rental companies
- Contacts at the home building stores
- Tool sharpeners
- Lumber suppliers
- Specialty tools suppliers
- Window and glass vendors
- Students (who can help part time)

For each of these contacts, where possible set up an account and ask for the contractor's discount. Establish an ongoing relationship to build trust among your network, and be ready to return a favor when one is granted to you.

NETWORK CONTACT FORM

Network Contact	Trade:
Name:	
Address:	
Phone:	
E-mail:	

Notes on work performed:

Special notes and precautions:

6. Marketing Tips

Here are a few final ideas and tips to think about as you develop your marketing strategies:

- Attach a magnetic sign to your vehicle with your business name and phone number.

- Have a sign prepared with your name and number that you can set out when you are working at a home. (Be sure to ask your customer's permission before posting any sign.)

- When you see a home that obviously needs some outside work done, drop off a flyer at the door and add a personal note regarding the kind of work that appears to be needed, saying you are the one to take care of it.

- If you have contacts in the real estate business, let them know that their clients may need the services of a handyman either before they put their property up for sale or after they move in.

- Advertise your services on the Internet.

- Send out seasonal reminders to your customers. Some customers may not know that you do all kinds of jobs. Give them a list.

Chapter 5

MEETING THE CUSTOMER'S NEEDS

You've advertised, networked, and made some personal calls. You have devoted time, thought, energy, and money to getting customers. The important thing now is to keep those customers.

Selling your service doesn't stop the minute a customer decides to hire you. It continues for as long as you have a relationship with that customer. To build the relationship you need to keep your prices fair, stand behind your work, and provide excellent customer service.

1. Estimates, Quotes, and Pricing

An important part of customer service is knowing how to present estimates and quotes to your clients. You need to learn how to balance competitiveness and fair pricing with earning the money you want and need to keep your business going. You want to avoid getting caught in the trap of underestimating in order to get a job, only to find you lose money on a job or, perhaps worse, having to later tell a customer that the job is going to cost more than you initially

quoted. Sometimes unexpected problems arise that can cause a job to take longer or cost more than you anticipated, and those situations have to be discussed with the customer, but generally you want to learn to quote accurately and live up to your promise of cost and timing.

1.1 Understanding quotes and estimates

Quotes are calculated documents that give the customer a complete and final picture of the cost of a job. Quotes assume that the customer has specified all the details needed to calculate the exact cost. You then add your price to complete the job.

A quote is generally not negotiable after it has been accepted; it is provided as a firm number. Often customers ask for a quote, but what they really want, and what you want to give them, is an estimate. An estimate is an educated guess of how much the total job will cost. It allows for changes in materials, extras the customer wants along the way, and so on. Estimates are generally given as a range. For example, you might say, "To paint the house, given two coats and some minor repair on the window frames, I'd say $1,500 to $1,800. It will be more if further repairs are needed and if I have to do three coats in places."

Estimates provide flexibility, but bear in mind that not all customers understand the difference between an estimate and a quote. One customer only heard the lowest number in the estimate we gave, but by the time she had added a number of additional little jobs, and changed some materials that required extra time to install, the final price was much higher than she had expected. From that experience, we learned that it is important to continually communicate with customers so they understand that adding to and changing a job midstream will likely result in increased costs to them. Nobody wants to face a confused customer.

Tell your customer what an estimate is and keep the lines of communication open throughout the whole job. Communicate with your customers periodically and let them know how the job is going and if the estimate you provided is still accurate. If there are any changes, inform them right away. By doing this you can avoid tense situations at the end of the job.

Sample 13 illustrates an estimate sheet that you can adapt for your business.

An estimate is an educated guess of how much the total job will cost. Make sure your customers know that an estimate is not a firm quote.

SAMPLE 13
ESTIMATE SHEET

Handyman Unlimited   Date:
10 Any Street
Anywhere

Estimate for:

_____

_____

_____

Note to customer: An estimate is an educated guess as to what the end cost of a job may be. This is not intended as a firm quote. As the job progresses, I will periodically talk to you about how the job is going and if we are on target. Please feel free to ask any questions you may have.

Summary of job (list of specific materials needed, coats of paint, equipment to be rented, etc.)

_____

_____

_____

_____

_____

_____

_____

_____

_____

_____

_____

_____

_____

_____

_____

_____

Weather and other factors

_____
_____
_____
_____
_____
_____
_____

Estimate: $ _____ to $ _____

Signed as understood:

_____   _____
H ANDYMAN UNLIMITED   Customer's signature

                                            _____
                                            Print name

1.2 What to charge

How much should you charge for your services? The objective of any business is to provide excellent service, cover your expenses, pay yourself, and make a profit.

There are a few considerations to setting your rates. First, calculate your expenses. What do you need to make in order to earn a good living? You should charge at least enough to cover the cost of doing business, which is based on your operating costs, or overhead. To determine your operating costs, make a list of monthly expenses. These will include the cost of your home office (e.g., utilities, phone, office supplies), insurance, advertising, taxes, and the amount you pay yourself. So, for example, if you calculate that your monthly costs are, on average, $2,500, you need to earn that amount as a minimum each month. You can then calculate how many hours you think you can work each month to figure out your hourly rate. For example, if you think you can work 30 hours a week (don't forget to allow for some non-billable time to do your paperwork, marketing, scheduling, etc.) and you can work four weeks every month, you can bill 30 x 4 or 120 hours a month. You then divide your monthly costs ($2,500) by your billable monthly hours (120) to get your hourly rate, in this case about $21 an hour. This would be the minimum amount you could charge to cover all your costs and stay in business. You also need to consider time off for holidays — so you may need to reduce your costs or increase your rates.

Second, you need to find out what other handymen in your area are charging so you can stay competitive. Check advertisements in your local paper to see if any other businesses list their rates. You can also call a few competitors and ask what they charge — you don't need to tell them that you are going into the same business! Once you establish what the competitors are charging, place yourself somewhere in the middle- to high-end of the range. Don't assume you have to be the lowest-priced business in town.

Third, ask friends and neighbors what they think are reasonable rates. You may be surprised at what they tell you. Often, the jobs you find easy and would price low are ones that customers consider difficult and are quite willing to pay a good price for. For example, you may have installed a half-dozen ceiling fans and know that it is a fairly simple procedure, but your customer may be afraid of heights and overwhelmed with the prospect of dealing with electrical work.

Find out what other handymen in your area are charging so you can stay competitive.

Find out what the value of the job is to the customer.

To this customer, paying a decent hourly wage for what you consider to be a small job is well worth it.

We have experienced this kind of thing in our business. At one job, Kevin was doing some front yard landscaping on a home when a neighbor approached and asked if he could take a tree down. The tree was small, less than ten feet high and about four inches in circumference. Kevin said he could do the job. Then the customer asked if he could also plant a new tree. She said she would buy it and have the tree delivered. Kevin agreed to do the job, which seemed very simple. He estimated it would take him no more than two hours with a built-in contingency. Before he could give a price, however, the customer said she was so delighted to find someone to do the work and asked if $200 would be enough! Value is really in the eye of the beholder. Don't underprice yourself because the work seems simple to you. Find out what the value is to the customer.

Finally, be prepared for customers to ask for discounts. You have to decide whether, as a matter of business policy, you will allow any kind of discount structure into your pricing. For example, if the customer is having a large job done, or you think they will have a lot of work for you in the future, you may want to offer a discount either on your hourly rate or on the markup on supplies. You can do some research in your area to find out what the customary markup is, but generally we recommend a hefty markup of supplies for small jobs, and a more modest markup for big jobs. The markup covers your expenses if you have to pay for supplies out of your pocket, as well as your time picking up and delivering those items. If you do offer a discount, let your customer know that it has been applied to the final bill.

1.3 Invoicing

Some small business people fall down in one of the most important areas — invoicing customers. It's easy to think that you'll take care of all your paperwork at the end of the day, or the end of the week, or even at the end of the month. But you especially don't want to fall behind in your invoicing. You need to keep the cash coming in, and you can't expect your customers to pay you if you don't ask for the money. Further, your customers expect to see the paperwork at the end of the job, so keeping on top of your invoicing is just another aspect of customer service.

At the end of each job, promptly prepare and deliver an invoice to your customer. State your terms of payment (e.g., payable in 30 days), and follow up if you haven't received payment in the time provided.

Sample 14 illustrates a simple service invoice that you can adapt for your business. Some word processing packages, and certainly all accounting software packages, provide template invoices that you can use for your business.

2. Scheduling

2.1 Planning for a job

Scheduling your time well can mean the difference between a successful business and a failure. The cost of your time is the bulk of the bill to your customer, so how you schedule your time can impact the cost of the job and customer satisfaction, not to mention your mental health.

Start your schedule with a clear picture of what needs to be done. You may want to make a list of what you need to take and supplies to pick up along the way. Sample 15 illustrates a simple form you can use or adapt to keep organized for every job.

Think through the job carefully, giving consideration to possible problems you may encounter, how much time each phase of the project will take, and what impact, if any, the customer could have on the scheduling of the job. Customers will often add to the job while you're there. For example, you could be painting the dining room when the customer unexpectedly asks you to hang a new light fixture, or fix a cracked window "while you're around." These extras are good for you and your business, of course, and you always want to aim to satisfy your customer. But too many changes can throw off your schedule and affect your plan for starting your next job.

You need to be able to balance meeting all the needs of the customer with your own business needs. If you can fit the extras in, you should do it. But if doing so is going to detract from another job, thus annoying a different customer, then you need to be up front and offer to schedule another service call to complete all those extras. It's always wise to build in some time as a buffer with every job. Plan for the unexpected and your days will go much more smoothly.

SERVICE INVOICE

HANDYMAN LIMITED
200 Any Street
Anywhere, WA 93307
905-555-0005
Fax: 905-555-0001

SERVICE INVOICE

SERVICE FOR:

JOB DESCRIPTION: _____
DATE: _____

BILL TO:

DATE	SERVICE DESCRIPTION	HOURS	RATE	AMOUNT
				$

TOTAL DUE

Invoice payable within 30 days

MAKE CHECKS PAYABLE TO:
Kevin Pegg

SAMPLE 15
JOB ORGANIZATION FORM

Job: _____

_____

_____

Customer: _____

Address: _____

_____

_____

Estimate given? _____

Date: _____

Items to take:

Items to purchase:
Advance from customer? $_____

Notes:

Here are a few tips to keep in mind as you draw up your work schedule:

- Be as accurate as possible in estimating the time needed to complete a job, and always allow for the unexpected. To be safe, make your estimate and then add 5 percent to 10 percent of the time as a buffer.

- Carefully consider how the weather may play a role in your schedule. If you are working outside and you have one fine, clear day to paint in a week of rain, plan on a long day to get the job done to a point where you can leave it. Very hot or very cold days may limit how long you can safely work outside.

- If you schedule several small jobs on one day, remember to consider travel time, billing time, talking to your customer time, and so on.

- If for any reason you are going to be late or cannot make it to a job, call your customer to let them know and apologize for the delay. Always keep your customer contact information in your vehicle and use it. Remember that part of being a handyman is solving problems for people. Don't contribute to the stress of your customers by being a no-show.

You can use a simple form like the one in Sample 16 to organize your time on one or more jobs every week.

3. Organizing the Work Site

Each job and each customer has its own idiosyncrasies. When you arrive at a job, you need to first evaluate the work site and take the time to prepare it to suit your needs with the least inconvenience to your customers. Consider these factors:

- Impact on the customer (e.g., noise, dust, safety)
- Power sources and availability to the work site
- Water availability for cleanup
- Storage for larger tools (e.g., saw or cement mixer)
- Storage for supplies such as drywall or lumber
- Parking availability for your vehicle
- Security for your tools and supplies
- Safety for yourself and anyone in proximity to your work site

SAMPLE 16
WEEKLY WORK SCHEDULE

For week ending: ______________________

	Hours						
Job and contact	**Sunday**	**Monday**	**Tuesday**	**Wednesday**	**Thursday**	**Friday**	**Saturday**

To provide good customer service you must communicate well.

All these issues need to be discussed with your customer. The customer may offer you a place, such as the garage, to keep your tools safe, or you may have to find alternate accommodation. In all cases, let your customer know what to expect. Don't just dump your lumber and tools in the front yard and assume they will be okay with that. If, during your work, there will be dust and dirt you cannot completely control, let your customer know and suggest that hard-to-clean furniture or items be moved out of the way. Give them a clear idea of how long an area will be inaccessible or unusable (particularly important if you are going to shut off the power or water for a time). Where you can, offer solutions to the work site problems. For example, if the kitchen sink will not be usable for a few days, help relocate dishwashing items to the laundry sink or bathtub.

The crucial factor to always keep in mind is that your work site is someone's home, and that home repairs and renovations can be tremendously disrupting to a family. When you prepare the work area, be sure to cover the carpets and flooring with drop cloths, and ask the customer to remove all breakable and delicate items. Move furniture, art, and all other belongings with extreme care. Always clean up at the end of each day with your customer in mind. At the end of the job do a thorough cleanup of both the work site and your tools. Leave the house the way you would want if it were your home. Always work around the customer and keep the impact on the family at a minimum. Consider that a family may not want you around early mornings on weekends, on work nights, at dinnertime, or when children are at home.

4. Serving Your Customers Well

The key to a successful business is satisfied customers. You may be able to fix anything, but if your attitude towards your customers is not good, you can be sure you'll lose those customers you fought so hard to get. Customer service follows a simple principle: treat others the way you would like to be treated.

But saying that customer service is simple does not mean it is necessarily easy. To provide good customer service you must communicate well, and that isn't as easy as it sounds. Many customers may not understand the work you do, how long things can take, or the expense of some supplies. If you don't take the time to explain the job requirements to your customers, they may have unrealistic expectations of both time and cost.

When starting a job for new customers, it is important to tell them your hourly rate and the approximate cost of supplies, or to supply an estimate, as discussed earlier in this chapter. Then, if they have any questions or concerns, you can answer them at the onset. The last thing you want is to start working and then find out the customer is not willing to pay what you ask.

All customers want someone who is trustworthy and reliable. Building trust starts with your first appointment. If you book an appointment to look at a job, be on time! If you will be unavoidably late, call and tell your customer that you've been held up. Reliability is crucial once you have secured the job. Everyone has heard horror stories of home renovations going on months longer than scheduled because the contractor disappeared halfway through the job, or of having to sit at home waiting for the handyman who promised to come at 11 a.m. and finally shows up at 3 p.m. Don't let that be you!

Live up to your word — and your work. If you promise to have something done today, and you are still there three days later, you will lose credibility. Don't exaggerate how much work you can get done in one day just to win a contract. You will be more respected for your honesty and good work, and you will be more likely to be hired back another time. Be respectful of the customer's home and life. For example, most customers don't mind if you listen to music or talk radio at a low volume, but it is wise to ask permission first. Using headphones can be a good idea when the customer is close by. With the need to make conversation removed, the customer can be more at ease with your presence. You'll also get the job done sooner without the distraction of conversation. Just remember to remove the headphones when you need to speak to your customer.

Don't forget that manners are always important. When you're dealing with customers, remembering your pleases and thank yous can affect your income. And there is never any excuse for foul language on the work site. Be professional, and you'll be appreciated and respected.

One of the pluses of running a handyman business is that you get to meet so many people, and if you strive for excellent customer service, you may find that your customers become good friends. Through the years many of our customers have become lifelong friends. It is rewarding to help people solve their problems and make decisions about their homes, and then enjoy the results with them afterwards because you've developed a friendship. Most customers

Be professional when you are on the work site, and you'll be appreciated and respected by your customers.

are very nice people, and if you're lucky, you'll have those customers — and possible friends — for life.

In a nutshell, remember these guidelines to serve your customers well:

- Be courteous and polite.
- Listen carefully.
- Recognize that you are a relative stranger in someone's home.
- Safeguard your customer's belongings as if they were your own.
- Be respectful of your customers' tastes and decorating choices.

5. Dealing with Difficult Situations

No matter what the business, problems arise from time to time. The handyman business is no different. Here is a summary of the most common problems you are likely to come up against, and some suggested solutions.

5.1 Not getting paid

Some people want the work done but don't want to pay for it. Fortunately, these people are few and far between. To avoid this problem, you can ask for a down payment or deposit once you have accepted the job and thoroughly discussed the estimated costs and expectations with your customer. New customers are taking a chance on your work and you are taking a chance that they won't pay. Asking for 100 percent of the cost of supplies up front is reasonable, as well as 30 percent to 50 percent of your labor costs. This will give you some money to get the job started and a sense of their willingness to pay. If the customer is reluctant to put down a deposit, and your instincts tell you the job may go sour, say "no thanks" and back out. With regular customers, you can feel confident to get started with a minimum deposit and then arrange a payment schedule.

When the work is done and you have submitted your final invoice, you should expect to be paid according to the terms you have specified. If payment is not forthcoming, call the customer with a gentle reminder of the amount owing. Usually, this is all that is needed. If the customer has a cash flow problem, offer to accept some sort of payment plan.

If getting paid becomes a sticky issue and talking to the customer doesn't bring results, you can take the next step of sending a registered collection letter on your letterhead requesting payment. If there is still no response and the amount of money is significant, contact your lawyer for advice. It may be worth making a claim in small claims court to collect the amount owing.

5.2 Damaged property

Accidents can happen. If you break or damage something, take responsibility and tell the customer immediately. Apologize sincerely and when possible offer to replace what was damaged. If the damage is significant, call your insurance provider for advice on how to proceed.

More difficult are the situations when something breaks that was clearly very old and likely to break on its own soon anyway, or when you find broken property in the course of doing a job. To avoid such situations, take your time when initially evaluating the job. Rushing may cause you to miss clues that some areas of the job will need extra attention. If you notice any damage, such as a broken window in the area of the job, or cracks in the ceiling below the job area, note them for your customer. Discuss, in detail, what you are to do and what damage exists before you start the job. Who knows, you may be hired to fix the items you identified in the process!

If, however, you find yourself in a situation where a customer blames you for damage that existed previously and was not noted by you, or damage that occurs that is clearly not your fault, you must weigh the value of that customer. On the one hand, if the customer is long term, honest, and worth keeping, you could offer to help repair or cover the costs as much as you can. This way you'll preserve the relationship with the customer, which may be very valuable in the long run. On the other hand, if the customer is generally a problem, you may be better off explaining your process of evaluating the work site ahead of time. Assure them that the damage already existed or was not a result of your work, and offer to repair or replace at your regular rates. If they insist on your taking responsibility for the damage, you can choose to offer a discount for the work to preserve the relationship or refuse. It's important that as an independent businessperson you recognize your options. As a last resort, you may choose to make a claim against your liability insurance.

As you gain experience you will feel more comfortable in anticipating the problems you may run into. Keep the lines of communication open with your customers and be completely honest with them at all times. Fortunately, most people are reasonable and willing to work things out. We have rarely run into a situation where we lose a customer as a result of damage on the job. If you build a solid relationship with your customers, most problems will be minor and can be resolved easily.

5.3 Family arguments

Any home renovation is a stressful event, and spouses and other family members may vent that stress in front of you. You may even find yourself in the middle of a family argument, perhaps being asked to choose between sides on how a particular aspect of the job should be done (not unusual in questions of design). Simply being in the customer's home can put you in the line of fire.

If you find yourself in such a situation, get away from it as soon as possible. Simply say, "Excuse me. I'll be back tomorrow." Never involve yourself in family arguments and never take sides. Resist the urge to judge and gossip about the incident and respect your customers' privacy.

5.4 Unhappy customers

From time to time you'll run across a customer who is never satisfied, despite your best efforts. In this situation, it's important to stay calm. Review what was agreed upon at the start of the job, referring to your notes on the estimate sheet or customer contact form. If you can show the customer that you have done what was asked of you, that should solve the problem in most cases.

Sometimes customers ask you for advice on things such as colors and style and then are unhappy with the result and complain. Watch out for this situation and try not to let it arise in the first place. You can make your best suggestions, but if customers are unhappy with the results, they won't be happy with you. Similarly, customers may not like the results of their own choices and still try to blame you. As a gesture of goodwill, you might offer to repaint a room, for example, at a reduced cost, or to redo the job charging only for the supplies at your cost plus labor.

If you build a solid relationship with your customers, most problems will be minor and can be resolved easily.

6. When There Is Too Much Work

Another aspect of customer service is knowing when to say no to work or when to ask for help. You won't be doing your customers any favors if you take on work you don't have time for, or if you try to do everything yourself instead of hiring help.

6.1 Saying no to work

As your business grows, you will learn that refusing work is not a bad thing. The trick is to know when to do this. Here are some situations that might cause you to turn down work:

- *When the job is too big.* If you work on your own, there will be jobs you simply cannot handle by yourself. You want to avoid being overworked, overestimated, and out of time. Customers will appreciate your being up front about your limitations. Pass the job on to one of your contacts and wish them well.

- *When you don't have the necessary license and/or skills.* If a job appears to need an expert such as an electrician, plumber, or pipe fitter, call the appropriate person on your contact list. Don't try to do it yourself.

- *When the job is too small.* A small job can lead to bigger, more lucrative jobs or to a repeat customer. But watch out for small jobs with big expenses for supplies and little opportunity to make money on your time. When work is plentiful, you may want to accept the small jobs for your regular customers, but otherwise consider carefully whether small jobs are worthwhile.

- *When you have plenty of work and the customer wants you to work on a deadline.* Often, especially in the summer, you'll have your jobs lined up nicely when someone calls and asks you to do something before a certain date. This means juggling all of your other customers, which you might not be able to do. Don't say yes only to miss the deadline and annoy your other customers.

- *When something just feels wrong.* We call this "developing your inner radar." If you get a feeling that the job might turn sour, stay away. Customers should look at you directly when you are discussing costs; they shouldn't be nervous, change

Motivate your employees to work hard and then reward them.

the subject, or otherwise be uncomfortable. If you get a bad feeling of any kind when negotiating, say no to the job and move on to the next customer.

6.2 Hiring help

When you can't keep up with all the work and you want to keep your customers happy, it may be time to consider hiring some help. Summer is a great time to line up a lot of jobs and hire a student to help out. Here are a few simple steps to organize yourself for hiring help:

- Create a job description.
- Advertise the job.
- Interview candidates.
- Select and give your employee a trial period.
- Set up a payment method and decide which benefits to include.
- Provide ongoing motivation and direction.

You may find that you don't have to formally advertise to find casual help. We have always had friends and family in need of summer job, so we haven't had to advertise. But if that's not an option for you, an ad in the local paper or a posting at the local youth job center will probably net you many possibilities.

Before you post the job, design a simple job description. What wage will you pay, when will you pay, what will the regular duties be, and what hours will you expect the person to work? Take the time to interview the candidates. Explain the job and the rate of pay, hours, and expectations. Ask a few questions about their skills and reliability and listen carefully to the answers. Select an employee with the understanding that firing is much harder that hiring. Take the time to do it right.

We recommend that you hire help on a trial basis. For example, let the candidate know that you would like to see how he or she works. Give them a finite job to do, such as helping you complete a short-term job. Then evaluate their performance. If you get a good, reliable student or other casual employee, treat them well. Pay them generously — at least half of your hourly rate. Motivate them to work hard and then reward them. We offer a bonus for employees who work particularly hard. For example, we might offer $12 per hour and tell them that if they work well, they can expect a bonus of $75 at the end of the week.

Make sure your employees understand how to work safely. For example, show them where the first-aid kit is located and explain what to do in case of an emergency. Be clear about your expectations when giving work instructions and let them ask questions. Show them how you like things done, where the tools are, and how to use them. In the process of helping you get work done, they are gaining valuable experience. Give them a chance to learn and keep an eye on their progress.

Keep in mind that once you hire employees, your paperwork and administration tasks are going to increase (see section **4.5** in Chapter 2). You may need to pay for additional insurance, for example. Consult your insurance provider or accountant to get details for your area. You may also be required to pay for workers' compensation insurance for full- or part-time regular employees. To avoid some of the added administration hassles, you may want to keep things simpler by hiring on a contract basis so you don't have the chore of dealing with payroll, deducting taxes, and fulfilling other government regulations. If you determine that you need permanent help over the summer or longer, then you can take the time to go through the proper regulatory hiring procedures.

Success in business over the long term depends on customer loyalty.

7. Summary — The Key to Customer Service

Success in business over the long term depends on customer loyalty. You not only want your hard-won customers to use your services again, you want them to speak well of you to their friends and neighbors. Here are a few tried-and-true ways to keep your customers:

✎ *Follow up.* Check back with your clients a week or two after you have finished a job to ask if they are satisfied with your work.

✎ *Respond to telephone calls.* Don't irritate your customers by not returning calls promptly. If you are away from your home office for long periods, check in regularly for your messages. Never make a customer wait hours for you to return a call.

- *Communicate with your guarantee.* Let your customers know what to expect if they have a problem with your service.

- *Live up to your proposed schedule.* Try not to disappoint a customer by finishing a job late.

- *Never avoid a dissatisfied customer.* Plan to meet customer problems head-on and deal with difficulties directly and honestly.

Long-term customer relationships are built on trust and fair dealings. The successful handyman respects the customer and shows that respect in every business transaction. You have asked a person to do business with you, to exchange money for your services. That exchange constitutes a contract, whether formal or informal. When you agree to the contract, you make a sale; when you live up to its terms and conditions, you have a satisfied customer.

Chapter 6

THE HANDYMAN AT WORK: ON-THE-JOB TIPS AND TECHNIQUES

This chapter provides some helpful on-the-job advice for the handyman. Whether you've been hired to paint one room in a new home, or improve the home security system for someone, you'll learn from experience how you can best streamline your work, and how you can give customers the most for their money.

1. Doing the Right Job at the Right Time

Handyman work is governed by the seasons, and it's important to take advantage of this feature in marketing your services. Typically, most people want the majority of work done during the warmer months. For example, you can't paint the exterior of the house in the damp of spring or the dead of winter because the paint will not adhere. But that doesn't mean you have to spend your winters wondering when the next job will come in. If you schedule jobs seasonally and advertise to your customers that you are available year-round, you'll likely be as busy as you want to be. You will also spend less time sorting out the right equipment and purchasing supplies because you'll know the kind of work to expect and what you need for several jobs in the season.

To get you thinking about how you will run your business and keep busy all year, here is a list of jobs that are suited to each season:

Spring

- Yard cleanup
- Window repair
- Sealing driveways
- Painting decks
- Laying patio stones
- Planting and general garden cleanup
- Assembling barbecues, swing sets, and other seasonal equipment

Summer

- Junk removal
- Exterior painting
- Deck, fence, shed building
- Weeding and gardening
- Lawn care
- Window cleaning
- House and pet sitting

Fall

- Cleaning eavestroughs
- Weatherproofing
- Duct cleaning
- Roofing
- Yard cleanup
- Raking

Winter

- Snow removal
- Hanging Christmas lights
- Interior painting
- Bathroom and kitchen renovations and repairs
- Installing closet systems
- Furniture repairs and refinishing
- Drywalling

2. Working on New Homes

You may think that new homes don't need any handyman work, but never ignore this important market.

Most of the work in new homes is painting. Homeowners usually want a change from the "builder's beige" seen in most new homes. Painting a new home is generally simple because everything is clean and fresh. You may find some small drywall nail pops, or bad seams and damage from moving, but there should be no major difficulties. If you see a lot of these kinds of flaws, ask your customer if they are covered by a new home warranty. Generally, most builders pay to fix nail pops, cracks, and general poor workmanship on new homes for up to one year.

Other jobs at new houses may include finishing basements, building decks and stone walkways, finishing trim work, and upgrading. Lastly, if you land a job in a new house in a new subdivision, don't forget to put a sign out. Advertising your name and number in this way can net you plenty of calls.

3. Working on Older Homes

A tremendous amount of work is available for the handyman in older homes. However, these homes definitely present more challenges when it comes to repairs and improvements. Each house has its own quirks to overcome, and you often won't diagnose these until you are well into the job.

Older homes commonly need exterior paint and repair, chimney repair, replacement of trim, removal and replacement of rotten

New homes can be an important market for handymen.

Older homes are a great source of business because they constantly need something done.

wood, and even the trapping of animals in the roof or eaves and repairing the holes left behind. Plasterwork also seems to be regularly needed in older homes. You might be called on to fix cracks and holes or remove lath and plaster that will be replaced with drywall. Often the small plaster jobs involve cracks or loose plaster in walls and ceilings. Over time the plaster dries and breaks away from the lath. Kevin generally tries to use drywall screws to reattach the plaster first. If necessary, he will use a washer made for holding up plaster, then tape over the area, plaster, prime, and paint.

If the house is very old, before you begin any work whatsoever the first question to ask your customer is whether the house is designated as a historic building. If so, you may not be able to do major renovations. In fact, you may need permission to paint the exterior, replace windows, or install outside light fixtures depending on the rules governing historic properties in the area. The municipality will be able to guide you or the homeowner if the designation of the house is in question.

Some particular challenges you may encounter when working on older homes include dealing with lead paint, asbestos, plaster dust, and molds. In these cases you need to be vigilant with your safety techniques and warn the customer that toxic substances may be released. Take whatever precautions are necessary, and get expert advice from the authorities when needed (e.g., for safe asbestos removal).

Needless to say, when working on older homes there is never a dull moment. In older neighborhoods news of a good handyman travels fast. Word of mouth is the way you will get jobs and many repeat customers. Older homes constantly need something done and they are a great source of business.

4. Painting Like a Pro

Painting, both interior and exterior, is often a regular task for the handyman. Many people know what to do when it comes to painting, but they lack the time, equipment, or inclination to do it. That's where you come in. If you follow a few simple steps and take the time to properly prepare your work site, your tools, and yourself, painting can be a great way to make a living.

If painting will be a part of your business, take the time to cultivate a relationship with the staff at your local paint store. They have a great deal of information that can help you get your work done fast and right. Some paint stores will give you paint chip books so that you can assist your customers with their paint choices.

4.1 Painting preparation

Preparation is the key to professional results. After clearing and organizing your work site, prepare the surface to be painted by scraping and sanding as necessary. Do any necessary repairs and patching, and then prime the surface to be ready for painting.

Take the time to mask what will not be painted, and remove all switch and plug plates. You'll save time because you won't have to go back and clean them off later.

Have a good-quality brush and roller with a roller pole. Recommend that the customer buy high-quality paint. Your work will go faster and in the end your customer will have a better job done.

If you paint surfaces in the order listed below, you will save time in touching up drops and edges:

Preparation is key to professional results.

Exterior painting

- Eaves and fascia
- Walls
- Trim and doors
- Garage door

Interior painting

- Ceiling
- Walls
- Windowsills and doors
- Trim
- Floor

4.2 Oil or latex?

If you're called on to paint a customer's house, you need to determine what kind of paint is currently on the surface: oil or latex. Sometimes it is very difficult to tell. For example, often trim will be painted in high-gloss oil because it is very durable, but high-gloss latex can look just the same. Generally, kitchens, bathrooms, trim, children's rooms, porches, and floors will be painted in oil.

Table 2 indicates the most common uses for different types of paint in houses.

TABLE 2
WHAT PAINT FOR WHAT JOB

Type of paint	Use
Flat latex	Ceilings
Washable eggshell or semigloss latex	Kitchens, bathrooms, bedrooms
Oil floor paint or latex epoxy floor paint	Basement floor, heavy-use floors
Flat to semigloss latex or stains	Outside trim and walls
Latex or oil, solid or semitransparent stain	Fences, porches

Paint stores have inexpensive kits to test the composition of the paint and they can help you figure it out. You can also try rubbing some methyl hydrate or rubbing alcohol on the surface as a test. If some of the color comes off, it's latex.

Latex paint can only be painted over latex, so if you plan on changing an oil-painted wall to a latex-painted one, you must first use a conversion primer, which is a special latex paint that will adhere to oil. It is available in paint stores, and by using it you will be able to successfully paint latex on the next coat.

If you're working the other way around — oil over latex — you'll be fine. Oil can be painted over anything.

4.3 How much paint will you need?

Be sure your customer understands what any painting job will entail. Take the time to explain that more paint (and therefore more of your time) will be needed if you are being asked to paint over dark colors, if you need to use a conversion primer, or if many repairs are required before painting can even begin. It takes time to do a painting job right, so be sure to accurately estimate both your time and the end cost based on how the customer wants it to look in the end.

Table 3 gives some general guidelines on how much paint you will need for common jobs. Keep in mind that more paint will be needed if you have to paint two coats or make a lot of touch-ups. Different surfaces and color choices can also have a big influence on how much paint you need. When buying five gallons or more consider buying in bulk. Five-gallon pails can be a good buy, and can also save you the extra trouble of many small cans.

Tips:

- When covering a dark or bright color with something lighter, prime the area with tinted primer. Ask the paint store to do it, or just add some of the wall color paint to your primer. Taking this simple step will increase your chances of having to apply only one coat of the final color.

- Remove oil paint from your hands with olive oil on a rag. It's not as harsh as mineral spirits.

It takes time to do a painting job right, so be sure to accurately estimate both your time and the end cost.

4.4 Cleanup tips

Latex paint can be cleaned up with soap and water. Oil paint must be cleaned using mineral spirits or Varsol. Use oil paint thinners for cleanup in well-ventilated areas only. Soak brushes and let them dry hanging up so the bristles don't bend. If you are taking a break from painting or coming back to it the next day, wrap your brushes and rollers in plastic wrap, and then put them away in a plastic bag. You don't need to clean them; as long as they stay wet they will be ready to go the next day.

5. Working with Plaster and Drywall

Doing plaster repairs and installing drywall may well account for a healthy portion of your work. Fixing old plaster and replacing lath and plaster with new drywall are much-requested jobs. Both plastering and drywalling take skill and time, and many customers are

TABLE 3
PAINT COVERAGE

Interior	Area	Amount of paint needed*
Small room 6' x 8'	Walls Trim Doors Ceiling	1 gallon 1 quart 1 quart 1 quart
Medium room 12' x 16'	Walls Trim Doors Ceiling	2 gallons 1 gallon 1 quart 1 gallon
Large room 20' x 25'	Walls Trim Doors Ceiling	3 gallons 1 gallon 1 quart 2 gallons
Exterior		
Small house 1,300 square feet	Walls Trim Eaves/fascia Doors and garage **Total:**	10 gallons 1 gallon 3 gallons 1 gallon 15 gallons
Medium house 2,500 square feet	Walls Trim Eaves/fascia Doors and garage **Total:**	15 gallons 2 gallons 6 gallons 2 gallons 25 gallons
Large house up to 3,500 square feet	Walls Trim Eaves/fascia Doors and garage **Total:**	20 gallons 3 gallons 10 gallons 3 gallons 36 gallons

*Amount of paint needed is stated in US quarts and gallons: 1 US quart = 0.9 liters; 1 US gallon = 3.78 liters.

happy to pay well for a quality job. Here are some tips for these types of jobs:

- Use a fast-drying plaster (20 to 45 minutes) and a heat gun if you need to speed up drying even more.

- Use as little plaster as possible to cover the area and do several coats. The end result will be better, and you won't have as much to sand off or sanding dust to clean up.

- Always use fiberglass drywall tape instead of the paper tape because fiberglass tape won't bubble and is more durable.

- If you have loose plaster to repair, or a hole in the plaster, the rule of thumb is that if the area is larger than four feet square, remove the lath and plaster and replace it with drywall. If the area is smaller, remove the loose plaster, fill the area with new plaster, sand smooth, and prime.

- Cracks in plaster need to be investigated to determine if the crack is from movement in the floor or wall. Ask the customer if it has been fixed previously. If so, you can go ahead and fix it, but the customer should know that the crack will return unless the structural problem that causes the movement is fixed.

- To fix a crack start by opening it up with a knife or pointed paint scrapper, then make sure it won't move by using drywall screws on each side of the crack. Tape over with fiberglass drywall tape and fill with fast-drying plaster, then sand smooth and prime.

- Before applying a second coat of plaster or drywall compound, make sure there is no sanding dust left behind. Plaster will not stick to sanding dust.

You should allow, on average, about six hours to install, tape, and finish 500 square feet of drywall. The amount of materials you'll need for drywall jobs are as follows:

- About 350 lineal feet of tape for every 1,000 square feet of drywall.

- About 30 nails or screws for each 4' x 8' sheet of drywall.

6. Plumbing Pointers

As a handyman, you should be able to advertise as part of your services small plumbing jobs such as replacing toilets and fixing leaking faucets. But unless you have a lot of experience with larger plumbing jobs, you should call in a plumber and subcontract the work. In fact, unless you feel confident in doing small jobs, it's best to get a professional to give you some advice or even do the job. You can cause a lot of damage if a plumbing job is done incorrectly.

If you do plan on incorporating small plumbing repairs into your business, you'll find it useful to keep some basic plumbing supplies on hand such as O rings, wax seals for toilets, plumber's putty, a plunger, and plenty of rags for the inevitable cleanup.

Here are a few basic plumbing tips:

If you don't feel confident with your plumbing experience, contact a professional.

- Shut off the water at the main tap.
- Close the sink drain to avoid losing any small parts.
- Wrap tape around the jaws of the wrench to avoid scratching the finish on faucets.
- Never start a plumbing job at the end of the day so as to avoid being unable to finish and leaving your customer without water.

7. Rules for Roofing

Roofing can be very lucrative work. Many people could do it themselves, but they don't have the equipment to do the job, such as a tall ladder, and they are quite happy to have someone take care of repairs for them.

In fact, you may be able to help your customers avoid a major expense down the road by pointing out that some "preventive roof medicine" is needed. If you have been hired, for example, to clean the eavestroughs or paint the house, you can take the time to examine the roof and recommend that it be reshingled or repaired, if necessary. Most customers will be grateful for your advice. It's a good idea to keep on hand roof nails, a caulking tube of "clear repair," and some black tar repair compound for small repairs. (Clear repair has many uses, from repairing flashing and eavestrough leaks to filling up holes in brick chimneys and patching holes in shingles.)

Watch out for these problems, which may mean a new roof is in order:

- Broken and/or missing shingles
- Old patches of roofing tar on shingles
- Protruding nail heads
- Smooth shingles with all of the granules worn off
- Water stains on interior ceilings
- Shingles that are not lying flat and have up-turned corners
- Large accumulation of shingle granules in the gutters

You might offer to repair the roof, but you should also be careful about recognizing your limitations. Generally, we don't recommend offering a complete roofing service. It's hard to compete with the teams that roofing companies can call on to get a job done quickly at a decent price. However, you can make good money doing smaller roof repair such as repairing a hole, replacing a shingle, or reattaching loose flashing.

Most of the work you are likely to do on a roof will be with asphalt tiles. If you come across metal, tile, or clay roofs, it's better to leave it to the professional roofing contractors. They have the right tools and the know-how to get the job done right.

Another repair service you might offer is installing a roof vent. Most older homes don't have adequate venting. In cold weather, the warm, moist air collects in the attic causing mold problems and rot. In summer, hot air builds up in the attic and keeps the house hot. You can solve these problems for your customers by installing more roof vents. If possible, you should install some soffit vents for the fresh air to come in and install roof vents near the peak of the roof for the air to escape. The result will be a cooler house in the summer and a mold-free house in the winter. The roof shingles will have a longer life too. If you are already doing work on a roof, you can attract some extra work by telling your customer about the many benefits of additional roof vents.

Tip: Install a roof vent by cutting a hole through the shingles and roof boards, between the rafters. Cut the hole the same size as the inside hole of the vent you are using. Fit the vent into place, nail, and seal with clear roof repair or tar, and you are done. If soffit vents are needed, you can use small round vents or larger metal rectangular ones. Install by marking a hole to fit the vent, sit the vent in place and secure. Space soffit vents evenly along the length of the soffit. Generally, venting requirements are one square foot of attic ventilation, both intake and exhaust, for every 300 square feet of attic space.

Also, keep in mind that roofs can be dangerous, so stay away from steep pitches, or very high buildings, unless you have the equipment and know-how to do it safely. If you decide to include roofing in your list of services, you must be very safety conscious. Some simple, commonsense steps will keep you safe:

- Always use the right ladder in the proper way.
- Wear boots or protective footwear.
- Always use gloves.
- Take breaks and keep yourself well hydrated. You don't want to be tired or lightheaded while on a roof.
- Trim back any tree limbs that overhang the roof to discourage the growth of moss and mildew.
- Avoid walking on asphalt shingles on a hot, sunny day. They can be soft and easily damaged. The shingles can also be slippery and dangerous.
- Carefully patch around weathervanes, antennas, and other attachments.
- Use a safety harness and tie off properly.

8. Yard Work

Offering yard work as a part of your services can fill in the gaps during less busy times in the spring and fall. Yard work can include a wide range of services such as raking, planting, weeding, trimming trees, cutting, aerating and fertilizing lawns, pruning, trimming hedges, removing junk, building decks, laying patio stones, assembling garden sheds, tuning up lawn mowers and other power tools, and more. Often the homeowner will have all the necessary tools, so you won't even have to transport a lot of equipment.

Here are a few things to keep in mind as you plan your yard-work service:

If you decide to include roofing in your list of services, you must be safety conscious.

⚜ Try to bundle services together for several customers. For example, rent an aerator for a day for about $45 and line up several aerating jobs. Customers will pay $40 to have their lawn aerated, but won't want to rent the aerator themselves. By organizing your work in this manner, you can make a good rate of pay and offer a great service to your customers. Rent the equipment for a week and your costs will go down even further. You can use the same principle for fertilizing lawns by renting a spreader for several jobs.

⚜ Cleaning up after yard work can be a nuisance. Use a large tarp to gather branches and leaves, which can be dragged or lifted for easier removal. Instead of bagging debris, we suggest loading it directly into an open trailer ready for a run to the dump or recycling depot. Branches and brush can be cut up in the trailer with a chainsaw (using all the necessary safety equipment) to compact the load, thereby requiring fewer loads.

⚜ Be cautious about offering to trim or prune large trees. This job should be left to the professionals. A tree service can assess the condition of the tree and the danger to surrounding property. Some customers think that trimming a big tree is an easy job and the cost should be low. On the contrary, tree service companies are expensive for good reason; the work is dangerous! Tree services are insured to cover damage from falling trees and are well equipped to handle the heights and other dangers associated with the business.

9. Taking on Wildlife

From time to time, you may be asked for help in removing an animal from a house, garage, or shed. Squirrels are generally the number one culprit because they like to move into older homes. They find a loose facer board or piece of trim, chew away at the wood, and before you know it you have a house guest. In the fall animals look for places to spend the winter. Avoiding having an animal take up residence is much better that trying to evict one.

Before there is a problem, you could offer as part of your services to check homes for loose or rotten boards and shingles where animals could get in, and repair them where necessary. If an animal has moved in, you can offer a removal service. Check the prices for other animal control services to gauge your rates.

9.1 Removing animals

To remove an animal, you first need to ensure that it is outside before you block up and repair the entry hole. Of course, first you must find the entry hole. Are there broken garage door thresholds that the animal can slip under? Is the vent screening on the exterior wall of the garage broken? Are there pipes that come through a wall into the house that need to be sealed up? Look at the exterior part of the dryer vent. Is it chewed up enough so that they can get inside?

Sometimes it is wise to temporarily block the hole and follow up with the customer after about a week. If they hear no noise or evidence of the animal, you can safely block the hole permanently.

If the animal is in the attic, you'll have to go in with a flashlight and investigate. Signs include animal droppings, wood chips left from chewing, and nests. Using live traps makes the job relatively easy. Small traps can be purchased cheaply, if you find yourself doing a lot of wildlife control. Traps of all sizes can be rented. Once the customer calls to say that the animal is in the trap, you should release it in an open area several miles away. (It's a good idea to show the customer how to set and open the trap. That way if the family cat is trapped, you won't get a call to come out and release the cat and set the trap again!)

Traps of all sizes can be rented.

⌁ *Mice and rats:* Traps can also be used to rid a house of small pests such as mice and rats. High-frequency emitters work well too. These units emit a high frequency sound that is inaudible to humans, but intolerable to mice and rats. They plug into a regular wall socket and protect your home from pests continuously.

⌁ *Skunks:* Skunks are common in many areas and they offer some interesting challenges when it comes to removal. Getting sprayed is something everyone wants to avoid. Skunks like to live under garden sheds, or under outbuildings with floorboards. They come out at dusk and return to their dens in the early morning. Set a large live trap during the day to catch them coming out or going back in. Bait the trap with composted fruit, something really rotten and smelly, and cover the hole opening and trap with an old dark blanket. Be careful not to cover the trap door as the blanket may get caught and not allow the door to close. The next day check to see if the trap door has dropped. Skunks have very poor eyesight and will not spray in an enclosed area. Take it slowly and carefully, and avoid sudden movements. Lift the trap with the blanket over it and transport the skunk to an unpopulated area. We use our open trailer to transport skunks and avoid having them in the van. Still covered, release the animal by opening the latch on the trap with a stick and gently removing the blanket. The skunk will leave on its own with no prodding from you. You may have to place the trap again if you suspect a family has taken up residence.

Raccoons: Raccoons are very clever and can take up residence in a porch roof or attic with ease. The animal must be removed from the den before repairs can be made, if damage has been done. To keep raccoons at bay, use bonemeal on the ground around the entrance to the den. They will avoid the smell.

Rabbits: Rabbits can eat their way through a garden in no time. To help your customers, install wire fence around the perimeter of the garden, and try adding Tabasco sauce around the plants. Tabasco is environmentally friendly and often effective in keeping rabbits away from crops. Recently it has been used with success by commercial farmers in Holland.

Wasps and hornets: Wasp and hornet nests are often found on the sides of houses or in trees. They pose a considerable risk for families with children. There are a number of options for the removal of wasp nests. Whatever you choose, bear in mind that wasps are not in the nest during the day, so you need to catch them at night. You can purchase an insecticide specific to wasps at your local hardware or garden store. If you don't want to use an insecticide, you can try to bag the entire nest, seal it, and leave it in a garbage can for a few days until you can't hear them buzzing. Then dispose of the whole bag. If the wasps or hornets are in the ground, you can spray with insecticide (again, do this at night) or pour boiling water down the hole. You can also fold them out by sticking the garden hose down the hole or trap them by hanging a flying trap in the yard baited with sugar, fruit, or beer. They'll be attracted to their last meal, as once they fly in they can't get out.

9.2 Pest prevention

All animals, including bears, deer, and coyotes, can become pests if they venture into populated areas and lose their natural fear of humans. To avoid the nuisance and danger of these animals, suggest to your customers that they eliminate the food source that is attracting them and keep their outside buildings clean, free of debris, and in good repair.

Keep small pests out by sealing holes where they can get in. Pests will not stay where food is short. Open composters are a veritable smorgasbord for the average rat or mouse. Pet food, garbage cans, food crumbs, and debris will attract and keep pests coming back for more. Help your customers solve these problems by building storage sheds for garbage containers, enclosing composters, sealing holes, setting and removing traps, and repairing damage caused by these creatures.

Keep in mind that you cannot hunt or kill animals without a license in most areas. In many areas you can trap small animals but it is illegal to relocate them. You will need to check with the local authorities regarding what you can legally do to remove and/or destroy pests in your area.

Here are some tips for dealing with pests:

- Use a mask or respirator when working around animal droppings. Breathing in the mold is dangerous and should be avoided.

- Wear gloves. Avoid direct contact with wild animals for your own health and for their ability to get back in the wild.

- Remember that most animals are afraid of people, so if you come across an animal that behaves strangely, it could indicate that it is sick, which means it can be unpredictable and dangerous. Call a professional animal control service.

Chapter 7

KEEPING UP WITH TRENDS — SOME IDEAS FOR TODAY'S MARKET

Current trends indicate that the handyman business is going to be more in demand than ever. An increasing number of older people are choosing to live in the family home longer. There are more two-income families than a generation ago, leaving homeowners with less time for household maintenance. The following are a few other trends we have noticed in our area that affect our business:

- Increasingly, municipalities are refusing to pick up junk from the curbside in their regular garbage collection, but families still have a need for junk removal service.

- Seniors are requesting regular help for small household chores such as changing high light bulbs, planting, and snow removal.

- Small organizations, businesses, and churches are looking for on-call handyman services.

These trends can be used to focus your handyman business. For example, you can market to the senior community by establishing a

There is an increased need for renovations that make homes more accessible for people with disabilities or for the aging population.

seniors' discount and setting aside a day or two a month to service all of your senior customers. Or, you could market yourself as a "one-stop shop" for the local business community or the neighborhood churches, perhaps even establishing a retainer for a certain level of service. For example, for a monthly retainer you could guarantee your availability to do emergency jobs within a certain time frame (say 24 to 48 hours).

This chapter highlights four current trends that we consider as growth markets for the handyman business: accessibility and universal design, home energy audits, home checkups, and home security. These may be areas you want to expand into as your handyman business grows.

1. Accessibility and Universal Design

As our population ages, there is an increase in the need for renovations that make homes more accessible. There are millions of people with a wide range of disabilities, and they often need help in adapting their homes to meet their individual needs. Developing some skills in this particular area makes good business sense and can lead to business with a whole new group of customers.

Barrier-free and universal design are terms used for principles that call for space and products to be easily used by people of all levels of ability. This may mean accommodating a homeowner who is in a wheelchair, or someone who is experiencing the effects of arthritis, decreased vision or hearing, or restricted mobility. Chances are that, sooner or later, you will be asked to make changes in a customer's home to make it more suitable for someone with a disability. It may mean lowering a banister on a staircase, widening a doorway, or building a ramp. Even minor changes can make a home more comfortable, convenient, safe, and accessible.

If you are called on to do this type of work, first take the time to listen to the goals of your customer and then plan the job. Also, when doing any job make sure you are not building in a barrier inadvertently. Consider how any renovation may limit the accessibility of a space and talk it over with your customer.

2. Home Energy Audits

Many customers would welcome information on how to save money on heating and cooling their homes. As a handyman, you could offer home energy audits that identify those problems that impact energy efficiency.

To do a home energy audit, start with a walk through of the home, make a note of problem locations, and then report back to your customer with recommendations on what needs to be done. Of course, you then have an opportunity to offer to do the necessary work.

Include the following items during the home energy audit:

⚡ Check for air leaks around windows and doors. (By decreasing air leaks the customer can save up to 25 percent in energy use.)

⚡ Check electrical outlets, switch plates, and baseboards for air leaks.

⚡ Check that the condition of any weatherstripping is reasonable and doing its job.

⚡ Check for windows that rattle. Where there is a rattle there is a gap and therefore a leak. Replacement or installation of weatherstripping may be necessary.

⚡ Check the condition and quantity of insulation in the home, especially in the attic. Advise if more may be necessary.

⚡ Check the wattage of light bulbs. Lighting can account for upwards of 10 percent of energy costs. You could suggest that 100-watt bulbs be replaced with 60-watt bulbs to decrease energy consumption. Energy-efficient, long-life compact fluorescent bulbs are another option, and they can mean huge savings in the long run.

⚡ Look for damaged siding on the outside of the house. Any holes should be plugged and caulked.

⚡ Look for gaps where pipes and wires enter the house. Fill as necessary.

⚡ Check for carbon monoxide detectors, smoke detectors, and fire extinguishers. Make sure they are in good working order. (Fire extinguishers have a limited life, even if they have never been used.)

⚡ Examine emergency exits, such as windows. Make sure they open with ease if needed in an emergency.

⚡ Suggest the installation of low-flow toilets and/or shower heads.

✓ Examine faucets for leaks.

✓ Suggest that water tanks and hot water pipes get wrapped to conserve energy.

See Checklist 2 for an example of a home energy audit checklist that you can use or adapt in your business.

3. Home Checkups

Many people want a thorough home inspection before purchasing a house in order to determine what work is required either before or after they move in. While home inspections usually require the services of a licensed, professional home inspector, a home checkup is a service you may be able to offer. For example, you may be able to help customers fix problems before getting a house ready to sell. Or you may be able to solve problems that a professional home inspector brings to light. You could even help customers stay ahead of the game by offering an annual or semiannual check on their home to be sure that everything is kept in good working order, and fixing any problems before they become too large — or too expensive!

Another idea is to offer complimentary home checkups for customers in order to solicit more work for the future. You can use or adapt the home checkup checklist (see Checklist 3) to keep yourself organized and to be sure you have not left any stone unturned.

4. Home Security

Home security is more of a concern to homeowners than it was in the past. It doesn't matter if you're in the city or the country, the general concern is the same, even if the specific needs are different. In the city customers may be concerned about main floor safety including the security of doors and windows, and night lighting. In the country, your customers may be more concerned about protecting their property with gates or fences.

Many of the customers we have dealt with on home security have been burglarized or are in a neighborhood where break-ins are on the rise. They want their home security beefed up so their peace of mind can return. If a customer calls immediately after a break-in, it is probably to request that the window or door be fixed right away. If at all possible, accommodate the customer and offer your sympathy and advice on how to make their home more secure.

Table 4 offers solutions to many home security problems.

A home checkup could help customers fix problems before they sell their homes or help customers solve problems that a professional home inspector brings to light.

CHECKLIST 2
HOME ENERGY AUDIT

Check Item	OK	Repairs/Concerns
Air leaks		
Doors		
Windows		
Electrical outlets		
Switch plates		
Baseboards		
Fireplace dampers		
Attic hatches		
Around air conditioners		
Mail slots		
Condition of weatherstripping		
Doors		
Windows		
Condition of storm windows		
Condition of storm doors		
Exterior		
Exterior corners		
Siding and bricks		
Chimney		

Check Item	OK	Repairs/Concerns
Foundation		
Entry place of wires and pipes		
Condition of exterior caulking		
Insulation		
Walls		
Attic		
Pipes		
Water heater		
Air ducts		
Lighting		
Bulb wattage		
Automatic lighting		
Appliances		
Seals on refrigerator, freezer, and oven		

CHECKIST 3
HOME CHECKUP

Exterior	OK	Work to be done/Comments
Driveway condition		
Exterior lighting		
Exterior outlet working		
Foundation condition		
Exterior surfaces		
Eaves, fascia		
Vents		
Window frames		
Window screens		
Garage door		
Interior of garage		
Outside structures (e.g., arbors, trellises)		
Locks on exterior doors		
Porches, patios		
Steps and entryway		
Yard condition: grass, bushes, fences		

Interior	OK	Work to be done/Comments
Floors		
Carpets		
Tile floor		
Laminate flooring		
Concrete floors		
Baseboards		
Walls		
Clean		
No cracks		
Wallpaper seams		
Switch plates		
Electrical sockets		
Mirrors, shelves, and other items attached to walls		
Doors		
Finish/paint		
Locks		
No squeaks		
Windows		
No broken glass		
No cracks in frame		
Open and close easily		
Latches and locks		
Tracks clean		
Drafts and gaps		
Ceilings		
No stains		
No cracks		
Paint/surface condition		
Light fixtures		

CHECKLIST 3 — CONTINUED

Interior	OK	Work to be done/Comments
Kitchen		
Appliance condition		
Sink and plumbing		
Conditions of cupboards		
No evidence of leaks		
Bathroom		
Fixture condition		
Grout		
Water damage		
Mildew/mold		
All drains		
Any odor		
Towel rails and other attached items		
Mechanical		
Ventilation		
Furnace		
Water heater		
Air conditioner		
Security system		
Phone jacks		
Ducts and vents		
Noise levels		
Other:		

TABLE 4
HOME SECURITY SOLUTIONS

Identified problem	Solution
Main floor doors	Use a good-quality deadbolt, with 3" screws to hold it in place. The 3" screw will go through the door jam and make it much more secure. Examine the doorjambs. It may be necessary to reinforce them by adding studs. Often when a door is kicked in, the door stays intact, but the jamb comes away and allows entry.
Sliding doors	Use a piece of wood dowel in the track when not in use. This is an inexpensive and foolproof way of stopping the door from sliding.
Basement windows	Suggest locking bars on basement windows, especially those windows that are out of sight. Just be sure to install the type that can be unlocked and removed from the inside to allow an escape route in case of fire. An alternative is to replace basement windows with glass blocks. They are secure, allow light in, and are energy efficient.
Second-story windows	Windows that slide can have a stop made of wood or steel to stop the window from opening,
Plant and shrubs around foundation	Suggest that plants, trees, and shrubs be planted away from the house or place them where they won't give cover to someone trying to break in.
Lighting	Lights on timers are great for when the family is away. Lights on a sensor that come on at dusk offer all-night light around your home. Lights on a motion or heat sensor offer similar protection and can save power.
Gates and fences	Gates and fences at country houses stop vehicles from getting in your driveway and getting out of view. Fences for security purposes are best at a height of six feet or more. Steel gates are recommended; they are light and easy to maintain. Wood gates can be very heavy and difficult to move.

5. Keeping on Top of Trends

Keep in mind as you run your business that trends change and new opportunities will always present themselves. To prepare to meet these opportunities, keep current by learning new things and watch for the trends within your customer base.

To expand your business and keep on top of the latest developments, try to regularly improve your skills. Your customers will be impressed that your expertise remains current and that they can count on you for the latest information. New skills also translate into new jobs that may be more lucrative. Look for learning opportunities at college or community night schools, at trade shows, at in-store seminars, on the Internet, or in books and on videos. Use your network of tradespeople to access information about trades. Learn about techniques and tools, businesses and marketing strategies, safety, new products, and anything else that interests you.

Chapter 8

BUILDING SAFETY AND QUALITY INTO YOUR DAY

Safety and quality of work and life should be considered foremost in any business venture. And they go hand in hand. You may carefully follow all the safety guidelines required for any handyman job, but if you neglect the quality of your life — getting enough rest, taking breaks from the job, remembering to take care of yourself — you may inadvertently introduce some unsafe aspects to your workplace. For example, if you are overtired, you're more prone to making poor decisions and costly errors.

Let's consider some safety and quality aspects particularly important to the handyman business.

1. Using Safety Equipment

It is critical to keep yourself safe while you are working. This is best done by using the proper safety equipment on the job. Your basic toolkit should contain the following items:

- Safety glasses
- Splash goggles

Take the time to assess the area for any potential hazards or safety concerns.

- Earplugs or muffs
- Dust masks
- Respirator
- Face shield
- Hard hat
- Steel-toed shoes or boots
- Gloves
- Coveralls
- Rope and harness
- First-aid kit

Table 5 outlines which types of safety equipment to use for different jobs.

2. Assessing the Situation for Safety Concerns

Before you begin any job, take the time to assess the area for any potential hazards and safety concerns. Don't put yourself in any unnecessary danger. Use all the necessary safety equipment, and call in the experts if necessary. Here are a few tips:

- *Lead paint:* If you are working in an older home, you should take the cautious route and assume that any paint from previous jobs has lead in it. Protect yourself! Use gloves when scraping and a dust mask or respirator to avoid inhaling the particles.

- *Asbestos:* Asbestos is very dangerous if the fibers are inhaled. Asbestos insulation left undisturbed is not a danger, but as soon as it is moved it can cause serious problems. If you are asked to remove asbestos, call a professional for advice. **Never** attempt to remove asbestos on your own.

- *Electrical work:* Evaluate the job you are asked to do and consider if you have the experience and knowledge to handle the job. If in doubt, call in a qualified electrician. (It also goes without saying that the power should always be switched off in the area where any electrical work is being done.)

TABLE 5
SAFETY EQUIPMENT AND WHEN TO USE IT

Type of job	To protect eyes		To protect hearing	To protect respiratory system		To protect face and head		To protect hands and body		
	Safety glasses	Splash googles	Ear plugs or muffs	Dust masks	Respirator	Face shield	Hard hat	Gloves	Coveralls	Steel-toed shoes
Painting with a brush and/or a roller	X							X	X	
Spray painting	X				X			X	X	
Sanding and/or scraping lead-based paints	X				X			X	X	
Sanding drywall	X			X						
Cutting concrete, brick, or tile	X		X		X	X		X		X
Cutting or sanding wood	X		X	X						X
Blowing leaves	X		X	X						
Using a chainsaw	X		X	X			X			X
Snowblowing	X		X							X
Power washing		X	X							
Junk collection and loading	X							X	X	X
Liquid chemical application		X			X			X	X	

Consider the safety of your customers, including their children, pets, and possessions.

- *Power tools:* Never alter the guards or other safety devices on power tools. Read the instructions before using a new tool and follow the manufacturer's guidelines. Power tools can be extremely dangerous in the hands of those who don't know how to use them properly, and danger still exists for those that do. Always treat power tools with respect.

- *High places:* Don't assume you'll never fall just because you have a great sense of balance and you have never fallen before. Falls can and do happen to the most experienced workers. Take the precaution of tying yourself off when working at heights. Use ladders appropriately (see section **4.**) and know your limitations.

- *Fatigue:* If you are physically or mentally tired, your reactions will be slower and the chances of an accident occurring will rise dramatically. Take care of yourself and get enough rest, take breaks, eat regularly, keep hydrated, and when you feel tired, stop!

3. The Safety of Your Customers

You also have to consider the safety of your customers, including their children, pets, and possessions. The best way to do this is to think of a customer's home as you would think of your own home. Show the consideration and respect that your customers deserve.

If you will be working in someone's house when they are not home, you need to ask in advance any questions that may affect doing the job safely and efficiently. For example, you'll need to know where the power and water shut-offs are, and if there are any particular areas in which you should not intrude. Be sure to ask if pets will be in the home when you are there and, if so, whether that imposes any special considerations. Pets should not be permitted to react to you as an intruder. It is not unreasonable to ask if a pet can be kept in an area of the house where you are not working, or perhaps be cared for by a neighbor or friend, so that you don't have the added burden of worrying about the safety of the pet.

If you are alone in the home, you'll also need to take special care to ensure that you lock the doors and reset the alarm system when you leave. Don't allow anyone else in the house while you are there unless specifically directed by your customer. We suggest that you do not answer the door or telephone while at a customer's home. If the customer needs to contact you, a call can be made to your cell phone if you have one. If you don't own a cell phone, you'll have to make other arrangements, perhaps setting a particular time to call on the home phone.

If children are at home when you are working, you should politely and respectfully request that they be kept away from the work area. Small children may naturally be very interested in what you are doing, but they may be putting themselves in danger if they intrude on your work space. Ask parents to keep children at a safe distance and explain the dangers of loud noise from power tools as well as any other potential hazards. While it is important to respect and be kind to all family members, you may want to limit interaction if it restricts your efficiency.

4. A Word about Ladders

Particular consideration should be given to ladders and how to use them safely, as it is the one piece of equipment you will be using consistently — and something that, if not used properly, can cause serious accidents. Choose the right ladder based on the guidelines shown in Table 6. (**Note:** Table 6 indicates the Canadian Standards Association (csa) guidelines. Other standards associations, such as the Underwriters' Laboratories (ul) or the American National Standards Institute (ansi), have similar rating systems. Be sure that the ladder you choose has a safety rating label from an accredited safety standards organization.)

TABLE 6
LADDER GUIDE

csa Standard grade	Intended use	Application	Duty rating (in pounds)
I	Industrial	Heavy duty	250 lbs
II	Professional	Medium commercial use	225 lbs
III	Household	Light duty	200 lbs

Look for the best ladder you can afford. Generally a grade II is sufficient for most purposes, although a grade III ladder is useful for light inside work.

- Common stepladders are good for inside and outside jobs but must be on a flat surface to be safe. A 6-foot size is good and can be folded and leaned on walls when the surface is less than level.

- A 7- to 11-foot multi-way ladder can handle more jobs than a stepladder, and still be relatively easy to store.

- An extension ladder of 16 to 20 feet is a useful size and will work for most common jobs.

- If you plan to work very high, get a 32-foot ladder. The 32-foot ladder is great for painting and roofing on two-story houses. The roof height will be about 25 feet, so the 32-foot ladder will remain steady with very little movement.

- Consider investing in stand-off arms if you regularly do outside painting and window repairs. Stand-off arms attach to the holes in the ends of the ladder rung and hold you away from the vertical surface allowing you to work on windows, eavestroughs, and other surfaces.

Tip: Tape a piece of carpet or other material to cushion the top of the ladder. If you fold it to lean against the wall it won't leave a mark.

To ensure you use any ladder safely, follow these steps:

- *Carefully read the manufacturer's instructions.* Be sure to use the correct ladder for the job. For example, use a nonmetallic ladder near electrical sources.

- *Inspect the ladder before you use it.* Check for loose or damaged rungs, braces, screws, bolts, and hinges.

- *Set up the ladder carefully.* Stepladders should be fully opened with the spreaders locked. For straight ladders, the locking mechanisms should be in place. The base of a straight ladder should be one foot away for every four feet of height. For example, for 20 feet of ladder height the base should be five feet out from the wall.

⚡ *Make sure the ladder's feet are secure.* If you are on uneven ground, use shims to even up the feet. Check the surface on which your ladder will stand. Make sure it is solid.

⚡ *Look out for power lines when setting up your ladder.*

⚡ *Don't reach more than two feet from each side of the ladder.* If you plan to climb onto a roof from a ladder, be sure it extends above the roofline.

5. Taking Care of Yourself

Operating a handyman business can be physically demanding, especially during peak times of the year. Often the work requires physical strength and stamina, with much climbing, lifting, and stretching involved. You must consider your body one of the most important pieces of equipment in your business, which means that to stay in business you must take care of yourself. If you are sick or injured, you will of course be off work for a time. Everyone gets sick on occasion, but if you take some commonsense steps to staying healthy and uninjured, you'll avoid unplanned and unwanted time off.

Consider your body one of the most important pieces of equipment in your business.

5.1 Staying fit and safe

Keeping fit is one of the "must dos" for a handyman. This includes getting regular exercise, eating well, and getting enough rest.

You may think that you don't need to get any exercise because your daily work entails so much physical effort, but if you don't balance the kind of work you do with exercise for the less-used muscles, you may find yourself very sore, or worse, injured. You want to be sure all parts of your body are fit and ready for any job.

We like to ride our bikes regularly to help keep us in shape. It's fun and, like any exercise, it helps clear our minds. Whatever form of exercise you choose, be sure it is something you enjoy so that you are motivated to keep at it.

You should also incorporate stretching into your exercise and work routines. Staying flexible and strong will help you avoid tight muscles and will decrease the risk of injuries. Consider any demanding on-the-job physical work just as you would any major physical exercise. Take the time to warm up the same as you would for a workout.

Don't forget to stay hydrated whether you are working indoors or out. Always have some bottled water with you, and try to drink at least two quarts (two liters) a day in warm weather. Take the time for short breaks as necessary to avoid exhaustion.

If your work includes lifting, be sure to lift properly by bending and lifting with your legs. A back injury could put you out of work for weeks. Where possible, get help for any heavy lifting or use equipment to lighten the load. Follow these steps:

- *Plan ahead.* Knowing what you're doing and where you're going will prevent you from making awkward movements while holding something heavy. Stretch before you lift.

- *Move close.* You will be a stronger and more stable lifter if the object is held close to your body rather than at the end of your reach.

- *Keep your feet shoulder width apart.* A solid base of support is important; holding your feet too close together will be unstable, and too far apart will hinder movement.

- *Bend your legs and keep your back straight.* Practice the motion before you lift the object, and think about your motion before you lift.

- *Tighten your stomach muscles.* This will hold your back in a good lifting position and will help prevent too much force on your spine.

- *Lift with your legs.* Your legs are many times stronger than your back muscles — let your strength work in your favor.

- *If you find yourself straining, get help.* If an object is too heavy or awkward, make sure you have someone around who can help you lift it.

- *Wear a belt or back support.* Always use a back support according to the manufacturer's instructions.

- *To change directions, move your feet, don't twist your back.* A back support can be very useful when lifting.

5.2 Taking time off

When you are in business for yourself, it's tempting to work all day, every day — especially at the beginning when you don't know when

ILLUSTRATION 1
LEARN TO LIFT CORRECTLY

Right way to lift

Wrong way to lift

To prevent back injuries when lifting, position yourself close to the object you want to lift. Separate your feet shoulder-width apart to give yourself a solid base of support. Bend at the knees. Tighten your stomach muscles. Lift with your leg muscles as you stand up. Don't try to lift by yourself a heavy or awkward object. Ask for help.

the next job is coming. But if you never take time off for yourself, your health and business will suffer.

Take the time to do a bit of planning. You should schedule your time to allow room for family commitments and leisure activities. There will always be unexpected emergency calls that will take you back to the job, but if you aim for a balanced schedule, you'll be a happier, healthier businessperson.

Don't forget to schedule time for an annual vacation. Most people need at least two consecutive weeks off to get a sufficient break, both physically and mentally, from the demands of work. You need to charge your batteries and gear up for another year's work. During your time off, try to avoid doing work around your own home — or you'll feel like you're still at work, but this time for a nonpaying customer!

You may want to plan your annual vacation in the fall or spring, instead of the summer busy time. Better yet, why not plan a winter holiday when business is slowest?

Whatever you choose, just remember that when you take good care of yourself, you're also taking good care of your business.

Chapter 9

LOOKING TO THE FUTURE

We hope you will enjoy running a long-lived and prosperous handy-man business. To do this, you must aim to continually improve your business practices, skills, product knowledge, and customer service. The world is constantly changing and so must businesses to remain competitive.

We suggest that you take the time each year to evaluate your original business plan. What has changed? Have you met your goals? What new goals do you have? Have you found a niche in your area and see an opportunity in which to specialize? Do you keep encountering the same problems? Don't undervalue the importance of thinking about these and other issues in order to continually plan for your business.

Monthly financial evaluations are also important. Take a look at the amount of money you have made and spent, and how many hours you've worked. Then, at the end of the year, examine everything together and be prepared to make changes. You may, for example,

Learn what your strengths are and have confidence in your ability to spot the jobs that are not for you.

find that you have been spending a lot of time on jobs you don't enjoy. Perhaps you can find a way to minimize or eliminate those tasks so you can enjoy your work more.

Here are a few common issues that arise in the first year of many handyman businesses, with some suggested approaches for changing the situation or solving the problem:

- *Need to expand customer base and find more work.* Think about marketing. Place an ad in the paper, post notices about your services, ask your friends to recommend you.

- *Need to improve skills to do more specific jobs (e.g., electrical work) yourself.* Think about where to get the skills you need. Consider night school classes, in-store seminars, or how-to books. Practice what you learn at home.

- *Need to find a way to become more organized; vehicle is a mess and tools are scattered all over.* Invest in bins to sort tools and organize your vehicle. Take a close look at how you schedule your work and allow time for appropriate cleanup and organization. Look for books and videos that offer tips on organization.

- *Financial end of the business is ignored; too busy doing the actual work.* Consider putting in a few extra hours to pay for a professional bookkeeper and minimize the amount of paperwork you do.

In the life of your business, there may also be times when you lack confidence and perhaps feel less than adequate. Keep in mind that this is normal. If you are faced with a job you're not sure you can do, think carefully about it and do some homework. Read up on the topic or ask advice from your tradespeople contacts. Sometimes you have to allow yourself to feel the fear and do the job anyway. Writing this book has taken confidence, and now writing books is on our "can-do" list!

Having a backup plan will also help you feel in control and confident. Calling on family, friends, and other handymen can be a part of that plan. Learn what your strengths are and have confidence in your ability to spot the jobs that are not for you. We all have our fears, but look back at your past and see how far you have come. You are able to learn new things, take on new challenges, and improve your life.

Starting and running your own business can provide you with tremendous freedom — and tremendous responsibility. By establishing your business goals early, sticking to them when they work, and adjusting them when needed, you will be giving yourself permission to succeed. Just keep in mind what is most important to you. Is it the freedom? The flexibility? The unlimited income potential? The absence of a boss? The challenge?

Whatever your goals, enjoy them. Explore, improve, and be energized by your handyman business — and you will be successful.

Good luck!

OTHER TITLES IN THE
SELF-COUNSEL BUSINESS SERIES

Numbers 101 for Small Business

Numbers 101 for Small Business is a series of easy-to-understand guides for small-business owners, covering such topics as bookkeeping, analyzing and tracking financial information, starting a business, and growing a business. Using real-life examples, Angie Mohr teaches small-business owners how to beat the odds and turn their ideas into successful, growing companies.

About the author

Angie Mohr is a chartered accountant and certified management accountant. She is the managing director of Mohr & Company Chartered Accountants and Business Consultants. Mohr can be heard regularly on radio with *Small-Business Survival Tips*. She is also a newspaper business columnist and has written many articles for business magazines.

Financial Management 101:
Get a Grip on Your Business Numbers

ISBN: 1-55180-448-4
US $14.95 / Can $19.95

This book covers business planning, from understanding financial statements to budgeting for advertising. Angie Mohr's easy-to-understand approach to small business planning and management ensures that the money coming in is always greater than the money going out!

Financial Management 101 is an in-depth guide on business planning. It's a kick-start course for new entrepreneurs and a wake-up call for small-business owners.

Bookkeepers' Boot Camp:
Get a Grip on Accounting Basics

ISBN: 1-55180-449-2
US $14.95 / Can $19.95

Bookkeepers' Boot Camp teaches you how to sort through the masses of information and paperwork, how to record what is important for your business, and how to grow your business for success!

This book will show you the essentials of record keeping for a small business and why it's necessary to track information. It will give you a greater understanding of the process of record keeping and a deeper knowledge of your business and how it works.

- Manage paper flow

- Understand the balance sheet

- Learn the basics of income statements and cash flow statements

- Record the sales cycle

- Learn how to account for inventory

- Monitor your budget and cash flow

- Understand transactions between the company and its owners

Financing Your Business:
Get a Grip on Finding the Money

ISBN: 1-55180-583-9
US $14.95 / Can $19.95

Financing Your Business will show you, in an easy-to-understand manner, how to raise capital for your small business. Whether you are just starting a new business or you want to expand an existing business, this book will help you to acquire the funds you will need.

Angie Mohr leads you step-by-step through the process and explores all the options available so that you can devise a financial plan that is suited to your company and goals.